YOU'RE GOING TO A HOME!

A Shocking True Story About Life in a Catholic Home for Children

By

John J. Diaz

© 2002 by John J. Diaz. All rights reserved.

No part of this book may be reproduced, restored in a retrieval system, or transmitted by means, electronic, mechanical, photocopying, recording, or otherwise, without written consent from the author.

ISBN: 0-7596-9836-8

This book is printed on acid free paper.

DEDICATION

To my sister Hilda

CONTENTS

DEDICATION iii
FOREWORD ix
CHAPTER 1
RIDE TO HELL 1
CHAPTER 2
QUARANTINED 7
CHAPTER 3
THE RELIGIOUS TRIANGLE 16
CHAPTER 4
THE PREFECTS 22
CHAPTER 5
THEN SUDDENLY JOEY DIED 32
CHAPTER 6
THE COVER-UP 42
CHAPTER 7
THE WAR YEARS 50
CHAPTER 8
MY CLASSMATES 58
CHAPTER 9
THE POST-WAR YEARS 65
CHAPTER 10
MY PARENTS 73
CHAPTER 11
THE AGENDAS 79
CHAPTER 12
THE END OF A SHAMEFUL ERA 84
CHAPTER 13
AN OPEN CONFESSION 91
CHAPTER 14
WHERE HAVE ALL THE HOMEBOYS GONE 97
APPENDIX 103

Acknowledgments

I am grateful to my family for their support and for allowing me to chronicle the emotionally painful travails of our youth. A past we have never discussed and preferred to forget.

Many thanks to my friends and colleagues who read, as well as edited, my manuscript. The advice they generously offered proved to be very helpful while I struggled mightily with the most difficult task I ever attempted.

There are no words which can properly express my gratitude to Theresa Kover for helping me, with her infectious positive attitude, cope with the mental depressions I suffered while reliving my tortured past. This wonderful lady devoted as much time as I did to the book, proofreading and recording the numerous re-writes without complaint. Her unwavering support and assistance was vital to the successful completion of my book God bless you Theresa.

FOREWORD

After many years of estrangement from my dear sister Hilda, I reconciled with her recently and begged her to forgive me for having misjudged her and for failing to realize that she is human and therefore susceptible to committing honest mistakes. God knows I've made my share. I also expressed my desire to write a book concerning our childhood experiences in the catholic Home for children where we were raised; and in consideration that she could conceivably still suffer from these memories, I requested her blessing.

Shortly thereafter, I received a letter from Hilda, wherein she expressed anxiety about my motives for writing this book and cautioned me against seeking vengeance. I answered my sister's letter of concern with the following:

My sweet wonderful Sis,

I can't begin to tell you how happy I am that we are part of each others lives again, and that I still have an opportunity to atone for my ridiculous behavior toward you. Behavior reminiscent of our stubborn uncompromising father and the loveless, judgmental harshness of the catholic Homes; reprehensible behavior that I previously refused to recognize as terribly wrong. Shamefully, I accept responsibility, as should my mentors from St. Agatha's Home, for the abusive treatment of the children in our charge.

It has taken me a lifetime to shed the stern, cold and unforgiving character, which I developed at the "Home". Finally Sis, I am now willing and able to express my affection, and unabashedly kiss and embrace my own children, who are probably still stunned by my belated declarations of love.

In June 1997, I found myself alone again and my newfound solitude triggered some deep soul searching. I was forced to face my lurid past, then I had to gather enough courage and determination to end a lifetime of denial. Suddenly I was overwhelmed with intense guilt for having mistreated so many children while in the Home, and I anguished over having caused so many people so much emotional pain – people who probably loved me sincerely.

Previously repressed thoughts of our brother Joey's shocking premature death at the tender age of two, now raced through my tortured mind. My liberated memory seemed to agree that the time had come to exorcise the demons, which had haunted me for half a century.

I now pondered about my role, (because of my delinquency), in forcing Pop's decision to banish us to a "Home." My thoughts were dominated by recollections of the childhood horrors we suffered and somehow survived.

These painful memories resulted in tears and self-recrimination, especially when trying to recall our unfortunate baby brother Joey, who never had a chance.

Then out of a clear blue sky, I decided to write to St. Agatha's Home for a copy of Joey's personnel file. When I received the file and read its contents, I detected some shocking discrepancies in the file correspondence. As if by design, I saw clearly from the Home's records, that negligence by their administration probably contributed to Joey's demise. Their correspondence also indicates that a cover-up of their negligence ensued. Obviously if it became known that they had grossly mishandled Joey's medical problems, the Home's ability to capably care for children would have come into question. After I finished reading Joey's unprofessionally prepared file records, I was beyond stunned at how ineptly the Homes managed their child care business.

Understandably Sis, these revelations aroused initial feelings of anger and frustration but I never entertained any thoughts of revenge against New York's "Child Services" Authorities. However, I do insist on accountability for any negligence connected with Joey's death. I would also welcome an explanation for the systematic placement of so many thousands of New York's children into catholic Homes, and the relative ease with which they accomplished their er—-goal?

The catholic Home's popularity was never more obvious than during the World War II years. One Homeboy remembers waiting in New York's Children Shelter for a year (1944-45) before room was available in the overcrowded institutions. I'm sure you remember when throughout the City's many ghettos you would hear mothers screaming the all too familiar refrain: "If you don't behave, I'm going to send you to a Home." It was a well-known fact that a simple signature from an unwitting parent admitting neglect or claiming incorrigible offspring behavior would free them from their parental responsibility.

I'm sorry Sis, but I must tell my story, and not only in consideration of Joey's tragic end but for all the other Home kids who also suffered premature deaths and many others who failed to overcome the almost insurmountable odds they faced in trying to achieve success or enjoy stable relationships in the "real world."

At this late date, accountability is the very least that society must demand from the architects of the crimes perpetrated against these unfortunate children, who were actually pawns in a greater scheme, where all involved parties realized their agendas with the exception of the "Home kids" – clearly, they were the only losers.

May God forgive them for their sins and have mercy on their troubled souls.

CHAPTER 1
RIDE TO HELL

It was a cold, damp winter's day on December 9th, 1943 when a New York Domestic Relations Court ordered that me and my siblings be remanded to St. Agatha's Home for children located in Rockland County, New York, and to remain in the custody of St. Agatha's until discharged in a manner prescribed by law. Two sisters of charity from the Home, who were impatiently awaiting the court's transfer documents, motioned for us to follow and we were quickly ushered out of the court and into a nearby parking lot. As we hurried to keep pace with the nuns, they abruptly stopped and opened the back door of a big black car, which would serve as our transportation to the infamous Home. My ten-year-old sister Hilda was first to climb aboard the car followed by my little two-year-old brother Joey, whose heartbreaking sobs were only interrupted by a hacking cough. I barked at Hilda to rock Joey on her lap, in hopes he would fall asleep. My brothers Georgie and Frankie aged six and four respectively, slumped angrily into the middle of the seat and I claimed the remaining window seat. The nuns settled quietly up front next to the chauffeur, and we slowly embarked on the "Ride to Hell."

It was more than fifty years ago and I was only eight years old at the time, but the memories of that fateful day have returned with shocking clarity. I remember well how relieved I was that the nuns made no attempt at conversation during the ride, because I was in no mood to answer any more stupid questions. I recall pressing my forehead against the car window, lamenting about my plight, and wondering how my rabid father could send us to a Home. Back then I could not understand what all the fuss was about. We were doing pretty good and Mom was receiving allotment checks from the Army – we always had plenty of food. And why was Pop so pissed off at Mom? He came home on leave from the Army a few days ago and argued with Mom, but hell that wasn't anything new. Aw who gives a shit, I remember thinking confidently, Pop after all, did promise to bring us back home after he finished kicking some Japanese asses. Then Joey coughing broke my reverie, and I peered over my shoulder to check out my brothers and sister. Thank God Joey was fast asleep – oddly I mused, he was able to cough in his sleep. Georgie and Frankie were also sleeping, and Hilda with Joey on her lap, was sitting back and staring out of the car window at the passing buildings with the saddest eyes I had ever seen. It was strange to see my sister so deeply distressed – she was always happy and laughed at everything. Joey coughed again and I shook my head helplessly and returned to my window, watching anxiously as we started to cross over the George Washington Bridge, slowly distancing ourselves from the exciting city that I love.

I remember how my mind drifted to thoughts of tough Tony, who was a big kid with unruly black hair, and the rest of the friends I left behind. I'll sure miss the good times we had on our (Simpson Street) block in the Bronx. I smirked while remembering how we raised hell with the cops, the truant officers and the Jewish merchants from our neighborhood, who were such jerks for leaving their storefront merchandise unattended and easy pickings for us thieves. I smiled recalling how a couple of Jewish kids from a neighborhood store tried to catch us with their goods and foolishly ventured into the darkened basement of a nearby tenement, which we often used as an escape route. Tough Tony and I crouched low behind the garbage cans and gleefully awaited our pursuers. As soon as the merchant's sons walked tentatively through the open basement doorway we let out a bone-chilling scream, leaped toward the startled boys and kicked them in their asses as they turned tail to run.

And I bet those damn cops from the Simpson Street precinct, directly across the street from the apartment where we lived, were happy to see me leave the neighborhood. They had a grudge against me, because I would shoot at them with my rubber band gun from the rooftops. We used discarded linoleum for ammunition. Well screw them I brooded, and screw the fat truant officer, who was too scared to chase us hooky players as we leaped from roof to roof. Sometimes we would elude "Fatso" by hopping a subway train to Coney Island and we would sneak back home after dark. My fond recollections were interrupted when out of the corner of my eye I noticed one of the nuns was looking my way, but she turned away without a word. So I went back to daydreaming and gazing at the passing scenery.

I was surprised to see how quickly darkness had arrived, and as night fell I began to experience trepidation and some serious apprehensions concerning our unknown, uncertain future. And now for the first time I was really scared. I remember fighting off the fear and forcing my mind to dwell on the fun times of the past year. Especially with the girls who would often escape from their apartments during the nightly World War II "blackouts", and find their way to my personal hideaway under the first floor stairwell of the building where I lived. I made it comfortable by moving the tenants baby carriages and cushioned the floor with flattened cardboard containers. Boy, I sure got a kick out of feeling-up the older (twelve and thirteen year old) babes who came to my hideaway to play games, such as doctor and spin the bottle.

Yea I thought, I was sure going to miss the Bronx, but I knew I would never miss my old neighborhood in east Harlem where I was born. It was there on the east side of Manhattan that Pop would force us to move from apartment, to apartment so as to take advantage of the two months free rent landlords would offer to move into their rat infested tenements. I cringed at the thought of how we used to carry our mattresses through the streets to a new home, every couple of months. After we moved to the Bronx I vowed I would never live in east Harlem again, regardless of the money I could earn shining shoes on the corner of Lexington Avenue and 110th Street.

Finally the car made a left turn off the highway into a narrow road, prompting one of the nuns to look back at me and ask: "Johnny, isn't that your name?" I nodded and she said: "Johnny please wake your brothers, we'll be arriving soon." I gently shook Georgie until he awoke, and then Frankie who's eyes opened wide and looked around furtively as if he had forgotten where we were. I could see he was as afraid as we all were, but I refused to show it. I tried once more to imagine how life would be in the dreaded Home, and I wondered if the horror stories my neighbors told us about them were true. But there was no way I could ever have imagined that my baby brother Joey would be dead within three months, and that the rest of us would spend the balance of our youth under the cruel and loveless guardianship of the catholic Homes.

CHAPTER 2
QUARANTINED

A short time after we exited the main thoroughfare for the final leg of our trip to the Home, we turned into a narrow winding road and a couple of minutes later our car came to a stop in front of a two-story white stucco building. As we hesitantly stepped out of the car, a nun dressed in white, much younger than the two nuns that brought us here, emerged from the building and welcomed us. A still sleepy Joey seemed startled by the surroundings and these strange people that he had never seen before today. He was reluctant to move so I had to take his hand in mine and urge him to walk through the infirmary doorway. The young nun then led us into an anteroom, which was painted completely white, and had two windows adorned with white curtains facing toward the front of the building. There were also several religious pictures hanging on the walls, including one of Pope Pius XII addressing a multitude of his followers from a balcony in the Vatican.

Two more nuns, who were also dressed completely in white, entered the anteroom smiling and greeted us warmly. They asked us to take off our coats and sit on the four available chairs, which were located in each corner of the room and wait quietly until called. Then one by one, starting with Frankie, we were taken to a room at the end of a small foyer for the obligatory shower and a short styled haircut. We were then issued long-John underwear with a large gaping (buttoned) opening in the backside. A trip to the kitchen followed, where we were served peanut butter and jelly sandwiches with a glass of milk.

After we gulped down our sandwiches, we were marched through a hall, with the nun leading the way, past a couple of bedrooms without doors where the only furniture consisted of a crucifix hanging on a wall and four neatly made cots in each room. I was bringing up the rear of our group and when I spotted a pretty nine or ten year old girl all alone in one of the rooms, I stumbled and almost fell as I gaped at her. She had long black wavy hair and dark blue eyes, and was wearing a simple blue dress while reclining on her cot reading a hard cover book. She looked up as we were passing by her room and when my eyes locked on hers I suddenly stopped and asked impulsively, "hi, what's your name?" She smiled and replied, "my name is Kathleen, what's yours?" "Johnny," I answered and blushed as I moved forward abruptly to catch up with the others. I decided immediately that somehow, if I could get away with it, I was going to sneak back to her room when the coast was clear later tonight. After all, I said to myself, I needed someone to get my mind off the many anxious thoughts that were bugging me.

When we reached the end of the hall, the nun opened a door and led us into the quarantine room, as indicated by the sign over the door. There were ten cots arranged carefully in two rows of five and just as the other unoccupied beds I had seen in the rooms across the hall, they had white sheets and army blankets pulled tightly around thin mattresses which lay on metal springs. Two old wooden armchairs that had seen better days, rested against the freshly painted white walls and the two windows were partially covered with (typically) white curtains – and of course, the ever present crucifix hung on the front wall.

Once inside our room the nun closed the door behind us and explained the meaning of the word "quarantine" and also advised us that we would be confined to the infirmary for a couple of weeks until physical examinations and medical tests were completed. She then assigned us one row of cots and before she turned off the lights, we were asked to kneel on the floor while she recited a prayer, which we were instructed to repeat after her. After we finished the prayer, Hilda and I tucked my brothers into their beds and only Joey complained a little before he gave in to fatigue and fell asleep – as did Georgie and Frankie.

Long after the nun, who told us her name was Sister Anne, put the lights out and closed the door behind her, I could see my sister was also still awake and lying face up on her cot, staring silently at the ceiling. I felt sorry for my sister, as I was sure she was feeling just as frustrated as I felt, but I had someone else on my mind who could surely lift my spirits, and her name was Kathleen.

Eventually Hilda turned over on her side facing my brothers and I seized the opportunity to slip out of bed and tiptoe to the door, then quickly opened and closed it very quietly behind me. It was dark in the hallway and difficult to see clearly, but I crouched down and crept one step at a time, being careful not to step on a loose floorboard, until I reached Kathleen's room some twenty-five feet down the hall. Just as I stopped to listen intently for any sounds of movement, the moon temporarily escaped the dark clouds and provided me with a ray of light which glowed faintly through the window and fell directly on Kathleen - illuminating her face, as it lay nestled within her coal black hair. I noticed that her eyelashes fluttered ever so slightly, an indication that she may have heard my nervous, heavy breathing and she was probably feigning sleep. "But what else could she do?" I asked myself. Obviously, I thought she was waiting for me to make the first move.

All of a sudden, I realized I didn't have all night and would have to move fast if I was going to act out my hastily laid plan. So I held my breath and crawled over to her half exposed face as she lay on her side facing me, and then I boldly planted a kiss on the softest part of her cheek close to her mouth. I looked up at her eyes for some reaction, but they were still closed - though I did notice a tinge of red had colored her face slightly. Then I heard heavy footsteps coming from the second floor above us, so I hastily crept back to the quarantine room and jumped into my bed. My sister, who was still awake, turned and asked in a whisper "where were you?" I mumbled that she should mind her own business and I turned around in my bed with my back towards her.

Although my short-lived adventure with Kathleen exhilarated me I wondered how I had the nerve to do something that brazen and I knew there was no way I could expect to continue getting away with it. I also knew that if I didn't behave myself I would never get out of this joint. Sleep did not come easy that night and when I finally drifted off to sleep all the apprehensions I had about our dubious future came with me.

As to be expected, that first night's sleep was fitful and somewhat scary, culminating in a disturbing nightmarish dream. However, before I could end the bad dream, my family and I were awakened by the blinding overhead lights and several nuns wailing, "time to get up!"

I slowly dressed and began to recall the terrible nightmare I had last night, about a guy (who sure as hell resembled me) that was dressed in dirty gray clothing with black vertical stripes, languishing behind bars in a jailhouse somewhere in Rockland County. There were mice running around the dank cement floor of his dingy cell which appeared to measure about five wide and seven feet in length as well as height. The bolted cell door, made of thick metal, had a two by six inch slot at just about eye level, and in one corner there was a commode without a seat that reeked of urine and human excrement. The walls were badly pitted and there was one small window with bars situated (purposely) too high to observe any passersby. This poor guy was standing on a wooden bench (that also served as his bed), in order to reach the window bars, which he was gripping tightly with both hands, and he was wistfully gazing out of the window at the stars. There was desperation and hopelessness evident in his brooding eyes. Back then I assured myself that the dream meant nothing and I certainly rejected the idea that the guy in the dream could be me; because I was positive, I would find a way out of this very real nightmare. No way, I said to myself, would I give up the freedom I had enjoyed for the last year while living in the Bronx without a fight.

After Pop joined the Army in 1942, I came and went as I pleased and I was confident I would soon be free again. I saw this as a temporary situation, which really caught me by surprise, I recalled, and I actually did not have enough time to find some way to avoid our impending dire predicament. Being uprooted from our home and placed in an institution was such an unpredictable and unbelievably drastic decision, that I could not then comprehend how this could be happening to us. However, I was positive I would be able, in short order, to convince my parents that our banishment to the Home was a ridiculous "knee jerk" solution to what I felt was a simple family squabble. But also in the back of my mind there was no doubt that if for any reason my parents did not reconcile, I would scream bloody murder until they acquiesced and liberated us from the Home's jurisdiction.

An annoyed nun brought me "back to earth" and curtly requested that I "please hurry," so I quickly finished tying my shoelaces and the nun marched us into the washroom. We washed our hands and faces, and brushed our teeth with hard bristled brushes and chalk-like powder, which the nun poured sparingly into our hands.

Afterwards while we were sitting at the table in the dining room near a window awaiting a breakfast which consisted of a bowl of oatmeal and a glass of milk, my curiosity concerning our new neighborhood got the best of me, and I slowly pushed aside the window curtains and struggled to see what I could of the Home's grounds. Unfortunately, it was still early and much too dark to see anything with the exception of an adjacent large stucco building to our left with all the lights turned on, which as I found out later was the boy's dormitory.

As I continued to squint my eyes with my forehead against the windowpane looking for signs of life, I wondered how many kids lived here and how many buildings there were in this remote (for me) catholic enclave. I had no clue nor could I even venture a guess about the logistics of St. Agatha's Home, or the kinds of pitfalls we would encounter there. Later on that morning I could barely make out a large dull-red brick building about two hundred feet across the road to our front, which appeared ominous on this dreary winter day. Thus far my attempts to check out the lay of the land had proved futile and it was beginning to drive me nuts.

My thoughts turned to Kathleen and our brief episode of last night, and I wondered why I had not seen her as yet that morning. I was anxious to see her and contemplated whether she would smile when our paths cross again. If she does smile at me, I thought it will be a sign that she approved of my brazen amorous advances and she will probably agree to an encore – only next time I'll kiss her lips.

Man, I remember thinking, luckily she didn't start a ruckus last night because I would be in some deep shit right now. However, I never did see Kathleen again, so I just assumed she was released from the infirmary earlier that morning and returned to wherever her classmates were housed.

Midway through the afternoon of our first day in quarantine, the nuns de-loused us and performed some medical tests in preparation for the doctor's visit. The doctor was summoned to administer the state-required physical examinations before my siblings and I could be integrated into St. Agatha's general population.

CHAPTER 3
THE RELIGIOUS TRIANGLE

During the weeks that we were quarantined, I remember thinking that maybe our stay in the Home might not be so bad after all. The staff of nuns who worked in the infirmary seemed to be pleasant enough, the food was not terrible and we were all housed together. However, very soon thereafter I would begin to experience first hand, the frightening reality of life within the confines of St. Agatha's Home for children; one of three Catholic Homes located in Rockland County, New York..

Although the catholic Homes of Rockland County were open for business as far back as the late 1800s, their popularity as group homes for children evolved during the "Great Depression" years, and continued throughout the 1960's.

The three Homes (Religious Triangle), St. Agnes', St.Dominick's and St. Agatha's located in the towns of Sparkill, Blauvelt and Nanuet respectively, were originally established to house orphans and runaways from almost exclusively, New York City. They included children of all ages and many nationalities, but predominantly from Irish American families of the catholic faith. Strangely, they also accepted some children of Jewish heritage.

The population of these Homes increased steadily through the years, reaching proportions upwards of thirteen hundred resident boys and girls, with the majority hailing from dysfunctional homes and negligent parents, and orphans were eventually in the minority.

Early on in the catholic Homes' existence, selected children, some as young as twelve years old, were forced to ride the infamous "Orphan Trains" for trips to small farming towns in the tri-state area and also in Pennsylvania, where they would be submitted to the careful scrutiny of farm owners. The farmers would pick the most able-bodied of the train's cargo of children to live and work on their farms.

By the time I was placed in St. Agatha's Home in Nanuet, New York, the orphan trains had long since been abolished, but the basic operation and policies of the catholic Homes for children remained intact.

St.Agatha's was comprised of some six brick buildings, three large stucco buildings, and several stucco cottages of various dimensions, spread over fairly spacious grounds. It included a handball court, a football/baseball field, separate play yards for the boys and girls, a few farms, apple orchards, and many acres of wooded area.

To the casual observer, this would seem like the perfect environment for any child to prosper, however closer observation of the Home's grounds and the inner machinations of their child care operation, would surely belie any lofty first impressions.

Some of the brick buildings including the ominous looking Administration offices and the chapel, were connected by covered walkways. The dorms for the girls, their school, play rooms, laundry and refectory were all located north of the chapel in an area completely inaccessible to the male population. Two of the large stucco structures which were also located north of the chapel, served as the retired nuns' quarters, as well as dorms for the white frocked Postulants (first year nuns), which they shared with the veteran nuns, who dressed completely in black – the official habit color for the Order of the Sisters of Charity.

The boys of school age resided in a large edifice a couple of hundred feet east of the chapel, which had separate dorms for each age group. Portions of these dorms were reserved for the many bed-wetters who were tormented unmercifully by their peers, as well as their caretakers. The toilets, washroom, and showers were located in the basement, and the Prefects were assigned private bedrooms on the first and second floors. Other solitary buildings included a school for the boys, a refectory, the infirmary and an unsanitary toilet in the boys' play yard. There was also a building which was named the band room, that was used for various activities such as: a movie house, playroom, basketball court, assembly room, visitors' room, and as a warm shelter when the Prefects allowed us to escape bitterly cold weather. The cottages were occupied by the pre-school children.

Routine physical exams were performed yearly, and dental problems were addressed from time to time. Eyeglasses were provided for the least vain, and those thick-skinned enough to brave the taunts of the bullies. They were called "four eyes" and somehow always underachieved in sports contests. Whenever I had an eye test, I would always cheat by memorizing the letter board and peeping with the eye I was supposed to cover - there was no way I was going to wear eyeglasses.

No animals were allowed on the Home's premises, and any strays that wandered into its confines were often stoned, and sometimes killed by hanging – courtesy of the more vicious and mentally disturbed of the boys. Having never owned a pet of any kind, I was not a fan of cats and dogs, but abusing them did not appeal to me.

The nuns served as administrators, schoolteachers, and nurses, supervised the girls, and weaned the pre-school children. Two male Prefects (ex Homeboys) by the names of Tom Maloney and Walter Kelly supervised the daily activities of approximately two hundred boys aged six through fifteen; a virtually impossible task to perform well, if you take into consideration the Prefects' deficient child care skills, and the troubled psyches of the children in their charge.

A third male employee (James McCutcheon) was in charge of the boy's refectory, where he conjured up cooking which was slightly more horrible than his caustic personality. He also ruled the boys' shoe shop and achieved notoriety for his steadfast refusal to replace the children's worn-out shoes until they were literally falling off their feet. Shoes with missing heels, and soles with holes the size of a half-dollar were often rejected by McCutcheon as unacceptable for replacements.

The children performed all the manual labor in St.Agatha's Home and toiled diligently on jobs that ranged from darning socks to farming. We were also made available to work on private farms in the area, especially during harvest time.

I'll never forget how badly my body would itch when I picked corn on the Home's farm. I would sometimes volunteer to pick beans for a private farmer near the Home, who paid us fifty cents a bushel. After working several hours under the hot sun most of us kids grew weary and quit picking beans as soon as we filled one lousy bushel.

The bulk of the funding for the Home's child care program came from the state and city governments. They also received substantial donations of money, shoes, clothes and food from Roger Peete Co., the West Point Academy and many others from the private sector. Clothes were often the children's choice of birthday presents from a visiting parent.

CHAPTER 4
THE PREFECTS

The problems and hostilities began from the day we left the infirmary to join our classmates, and continued throughout my tumultuous nine-plus years under the guardianship of the catholic Homes. On that first unforgettable evening I was sitting at a dinner table in the refectory with five of my classmates when the nun who was supervising the meal hovered menacingly over the back of my chair. Annoyed that I was slouched in my seat, sulking and ignoring the food on my plate, the nun curtly told me to "sit up straight and finish eating." I had eaten the lousy spaghetti because I was hungry but I had never even seen spinach, nor did I like how it smelled – so I refused. The angry nun pulled the short hair on my head back, forcing my mouth open, and tried her best to stuff a spoon-full of the tasteless, stringy vegetable down my throat, and I promptly puked all over the floor – and her shoes. She then grabbed one of my ears with the thumb and forefinger of her hand, pulled me upright and rushed me into the washroom.

After I finished cleaning my face and shirt with toilet paper and ice cold water, I was greeted at the washroom door by the still furious nun, who threw a rag at my face and ordered me to wipe the vomit off the floor.

That night I lay on my bunk, pulled the worn-out army blanket over my head, and cried myself to sleep. The first of many nights that my frustration with the heartless and brutal treatment at St. Agatha's Home would anger me to tears.

The following day I was assigned to work in the refectory for James McCutcheon, one of the three male Prefects employed by the Home, who became my worst nightmare. For some reason I was not one of his favorite employees and he would seize every opportunity to critique my work ethics.

James McCutcheon and his fellow Prefects, Walter Kelly and Tom Maloney, were as physically diverse as any three men could possibly be, but that is where their differences ended. They all gave credence to the premise that total control was attainable through fear only, and they unilaterally believed that corporal punishment was the necessary instrument to that end. All three had terrible tempers, which flared up on a daily basis.

Every misdeed from the most trifling, such as gazing out the window, was punishable by an angry Prefect wielding a stickball bat. The quantity of blows from the bat was dependent on the severity of the infraction, and the kids were sometimes mercifully allowed the option of choosing which body part (hands or butt) they wished to sacrifice. When exacting spur-of-the-moment discipline the Prefects would invariably resort to using their fists and feet.

Being an adventurous and daring soul, I was often on the receiving end of punches and kicks. I vividly remember sporting a black eye for a couple of weeks in 1945, after failing to duck when Mr. Kelly sucker-punched me.

As improbable as it may seem, the cruel and violent punishment meted out by the Home's Prefects carried the blessings of the good Sisters of Charity. The nuns corroborated with the Prefects in their vicious assaults on the children, by supplying them with the names of the sinners and their offenses on a weekly basis.

JAMES MCCUTCHEON was a bald-headed, fiftyish man of medium height, with a thick neck, big ass, and a grossly oversized waist. He had a violent temper and a booming voice that carried from one end of the Home to the other. If he called your name, you had better come running, or there would be hell to pay. When exacting punishment, he would use any available weapon within his grasp to pummel the defenseless children.

I can still remember the time McCutcheon chased a kid off the shoe inspection line, while brandishing an iron pipe, because he suspected the guy of enhancing his shoes' defective soles in order to exchange them for a new pair. I was on the shoe line that day and I recall feeling gratified that the accused kid was able to duck, and he only suffered a glancing blow from McCutcheon's weapon, to go along with that terrified look on his face. Several horrified boys and I decided to bolt the shoe line immediately, rather than run the risk of facing a similar reaction from his "His Fatness" after examining our border-line defective shoes.

Taking a blow on the head from McCutcheon with a shoe was an acceptable trade-off for replacements, but chancing a piping would have been foolhardy to say the least. McCutcheon somehow could never understand how the condition of our shoes deteriorated so quickly, despite knowing very well that we wore them for all our daily activities from playing handball, football, and baseball, to attending Mass services.

WALTER KELLY – derisively referred to as "Spud Chest," was a short, oddly shaped gnome of a man with inordinately long arms and an oversized head. In as much as he was an ex-Home boy, who doubtlessly endured cruel jokes and taunts from his Home brethren, it should not be difficult to ascertain how Spud Chest developed a personality totally devoid of compassion and sensitivity.

I can also honestly say that during my five and a half years in St. Agatha's Home, I never saw the 30 odd-year-old Kelly with a smile on his face. His refusal to acknowledge humorous situations brings to mind an incident that occurred during one of our infrequent showers, and which everyone but Mr. Kelly found amusing.

Approximately 25 eight and nine-year-old boys from my third grade class, were crowded into a small shower room where complete silence was the absolute rule. After wetting the boys down Mr. Kelly ordered us to turn off the water, and we quickly began soaping our bodies with the few available huge, brown colored rock-hard bars of soap, when suddenly the faint sound of a monotone hum broke the silence. Mr. Kelly slowly rose from his nearby chair, and in a deliberate manner demanded that the guilty hummingbird step forward, and admit to disobeyance of the "rule of silence" while showering - though not exactly in that language. While Kelly waited for the perp to "give himself up," he was banging a sawed-off stickball bat menacingly against his hand. A boy named Romeo, who we all knew had a nervous humming habit was too afraid to confess, and the rest of us would never think of ratting on a classmate. Mr. Kelly's face reddened and he sat down on his chair, staring intently into the shower room.

The air was becoming increasingly tense, and poor, scared Romeo reacted with another uncontrollable, "Hummm." A visibly agitated Kelly leaped to his feet, and facing the concerned boys, he asked in an even, determined voice: "Who's the wise guy that's doing the humming? If the guy doesn't own up, everybody gets hit on the way out of the shower," he continued. With that, several boys located near the rear of the room feared they were standing too close to Romeo for comfort and edged away – so as not to become victims of mistaken identity. Kelly glared at the now exposed Romeo and shouted angrily, "was that you Romeo?" A terrified Romeo yelled back, "not me Mr. Kelly - Hummm!" While everyone fought to keep from flat-out laughing aloud, Kelly fumed and we all paid dearly on the way out of the shower room, with two blows each from his bat, across our outstretched hands.

Mr. Kelly actually preferred using his fists on children who misbehaved. He enjoyed circling his victims, and would intermittently throw his shoulders back while berating them for their transgressions. Then suddenly, without warning, one of his low hanging fists (below his knees) would lash out swiftly toward the unsuspecting child's head. Nice guy – Mr. Kelly.

TOM MALONEY was a slightly overweight man of medium height who appeared to be in his late thirties. He had average good looks, slicked-back red hair and piercing blue eyes. Maloney was an impeccably dressed individual, who favored gabardine pants and expensive shirts and jackets in colors that always complimented his fair complexion and red hair. His shoes were always well shined, and he was never seen unshaven, or wearing dungaree trousers. He had a quick, confident gait and he always seemed to charm the nuns who crossed his path. If the nuns stopped to exchange pleasantries with Tom, they would invariably giggle and blush like teenage girls.

However, Maloney had a curious and maddening habit of jingling the ever-present coins in his pants' pockets. Considering the fact that the nearest retail stores were miles away, and coin operated telephones and soda machines were non-existent, why I wondered, did he need a pocket-full of change? I also wondered why I never saw him in the company of a woman, but then, I never saw any Prefect with a female companion.

The Home's administrator assigned Tom a host of duties which included supervision of the older (10-15 year old) boys, Coach of the ball teams, conductor of the choir and chorus, and director of the theatrical plays performed by the children. He handled his duties in a capable manner, with the exception of supervising the boys' daily activities. In this, the most important of his responsibilities, he failed miserably.

The man lacked patience, understanding and compassion, and he possessed a short, vicious temper - directly attributable to the heavy workload he carried. Somehow his employers were oblivious of the dangerous climate they created in their institution by over-working their

Prefects, or perhaps they chose to ignore the consequences after weighing them against fiscal consideration.

Although Maloney subscribed to corporal punishment, he also found it distasteful on a daily basis, that is. He subsequently decreed that the children in his charge, who were caught misbehaving, would be dealt with severely one night per week only. He further decreed that the "night of reckoning" would be on Thursday of each week, and would henceforth be known as (strangely) "Brick night" – or the night Maloney would throw the bricks at us. He kept a list of the juvenile offenders, which included the names submitted by the nuns, and he also decided the amount of punishment each misdeed deserved. As I now recall the unfair brutality of Maloney's "brick nights" a haunting memory returns concerning one such Thursday night in which I played a reluctant part.

The year was 1947, and I was in the sixth grade classroom of Sister Leo, a pale, sickly looking nun with a slight build and a cold, vindictive, and heartless personality. While Sister Leo was writing on the classroom blackboard one day, I seized the opportunity to send a spitball flying toward the head of a classmate by the name of Bobby Casanova, who sat in the first row. Just as Casanova was returning the spitball toward the general area of my desk, Sister Leo turned around and unfortunately caught him in the act. For this ungodly deed, poor Cassie was the recipient of fifty whacks across his butt from Maloney armed with a stickball bat. I remember wincing after every blow landed, and I was haunted for years afterward by the heart-wrenching muffled sobs emanating from Cassie's bunk bed throughout that unforgettable Thursday night.

I will always admire Cassie for upholding the unwritten code, which forbade ratting on a classmate and for refusing to cry or plead for mercy while the assault was in progress. I felt an intense hatred for Maloney that night and swore I would beat the hell out of him when I grew up.

My chance for revenge came twenty-five years later at the only reunion of St. Agatha's alumni I ever attended. But alas, Tom Maloney who also showed up was confined to a wheelchair. He had suffered a stroke and did not even recognize me. Under the circumstances, breaking his jaw would have served no purpose, so I contented myself with the knowledge that he would be a vegetable, imprisoned in an iron horse for the rest of his life. That day I buried my hate for Maloney, but I refused to feel any remorse for him.

It certainly is fair to say that the Home's Prefects were totally unqualified for the positions they held for so many years. I also dare say that in today's world the Prefects would be labeled sociopaths and arrested by the State's District Attorney on child abuse charges – a felony!

Admittedly throughout much of my internment at the Homes' and for many years thereafter I was also an advocate of using the austere, no tolerance system in rearing children - practiced to perfection by St. Agatha's administration. I deeply regret occasionally abusing the children in my charge when I was a teenager in St. Agnes' Home.

CHAPTER 5
THEN SUDDENLY JOEY DIED

As the days slowly passed, during our first winter in the Home I became increasingly despondent, and remember that I even considered running away, but I persevered because I couldn't consciously desert my sister and brothers - and they sure as hell would not be able to walk the twenty seven miles to New York City.

My brothers Georgie and Frankie were handling our transition as well as could be expected, however little Joey was spending too much time in the Home's infirmary. He couldn't seem to kick the nagging cough that had been hanging on for months, and his nose was constantly running. I remember being really worried about Joey's health, but even more about my sister Hilda, who was having all kinds of problems with the nuns.

My sister and I used to meet on Sundays after mass, and trade "war stories." I still remember some of her harrowing stories about the corporal punishment and abject cruelty she experienced at the hands of the nuns.

One such story involved a ten-year old girl who was my sister's classmate and good friend. Unfortunately Hilda's friend, a bed-wetter, had stained her mattress with urine the previous night, and an irate Sister Joseph was chastising her unmercifully. Apparently the rubber sheet, which should have covered the young girl's mattress completely, had shifted while she slept leaving the mattress partially exposed. My sister was unable to stand by any longer and watch while her humiliated friend cried and cowered under the nun's fierce verbal abuse; so she stepped boldly in front of her friend like a knight's shield and heatedly voiced her objections to the nun, who promptly smacked Hilda sending her halfway across the room on her butt. The nun then added insult to injury by forcing Hilda to sleep with the bed-wetter the following night, thereby assuring my sister of a torturous night soaked in cold urine.

Almost three months had passed since we first set foot on the Home grounds and I was still plagued with constant bouts of depression. The Prefects were trying awfully hard to knock the chip off my shoulder and break my spirit. But I sucked it up defiantly, and held on to my steadfast belief that my father would fulfill his promise to liberate us from the Home as soon as the war was over.

Then just when I thought my life could not possibly become more unbearable, my siblings and I were dealt the most severe emotional blow we would ever suffer. Suddenly Joey died.

Our gorgeous baby brother, who had curly brown hair, hazel eyes with long lashes and a beautiful smile, passed away on a cold and rainy seventh day of March 1944 in New York City's Bellevue Hospital.

Joey was a sweet, lovable child, and the pride and joy of our family. I remember how we used to carry him around like a precious trophy and people walking the streets of New York would often stop to look at him in wonder and exclaim: "What a beautiful child." Others would do a "double take" after catching a glimpse of Joey as we passed them by.

Friends of our family would constantly warn us not to spoil him, but we didn't listen. Especially Hilda, who spoiled him shamelessly and treated him like a doting mother.

Joey's tragic death so devastated my family that we never discussed his passing, as obviously it was much too painful a subject to broach. We loved that little dude.

Throughout my life I was able to fight off the memory of Joey's death by using the many distractions the world offered me. But suddenly in June 1997 without warning, I found myself alone, in the twilight of my life and without any of the previously available distractions to occupy my mind. I was no longer able to avoid facing my unwanted past. No matter how hard I tried, I was unable to fight off the terrible memories which prominently featured my baby brother's death. Then one day in late July 1997 I finally accepted the inevitable and decided that the time had come to bring Joey's death to closure. Surely I thought, this deep introspection which I previously spurned is the genesis of the solitude I was now experiencing.

However, seeking closure to any tragedy is easier said than done, and confronting the worst emotional trauma of my sixty-five years on this planet proved more difficult than I could have imagined. I shed a lot of tears and that was understandable but as the days passed into weeks then months, the uncontrollable limpid fluid still flowed inevitably from my eyes whenever I thought about Joey, or saw his name in print.

This inability to control my emotions was very disconcerting, to say the least, and to make matters worse I foolishly began to drink vodka in excess, which resulted in loss of sleep and a diminished appetite.

Finally, predicated by desperation and a farfetched idea, I decided to write to St. Agatha's Home and request that they send me a copy of Joey's personnel file. For some reason, my mind felt that perhaps familiarizing myself with the circumstances surrounding his death would hopefully help "stop the bleeding" in my aching heart. A long shot I thought, but at this point, anything was worth a try as I was at my wits end.

It was the ninth day of October 1997, and two weeks had passed since I wrote a letter to St.Agatha's Home wherein I requested copies of Joey's personnel file, and I was becoming a little concerned about the availability of the files (due to their age) as well as the Home's willingness to part with them. Therefore I wasn't too optimistic when I went down to check my mailbox that day. But when I saw the manila envelope with the Home's return address, I smiled and climbed the flight of stairs hurriedly (two steps at a time) up to my apartment, ripped open one end of the envelope and pulled out the cover letter. The letter simply advised me that along with the copies of Joey's records they also included photostats of my file – a touch of surprising sensitivity, I thought.

Then as I began to examine the contents of the file I was overwhelmed with sadness and could not continue reading the sorrowful accounts of my brother's death, so I put the papers back inside the envelope and buried it in my dresser drawer out of sight.

A few days later, I was finally able to utter Joey's name and think about him without fighting the tears. The sadness I first experienced was replaced by strange feelings, which seemed to bring me closer to him, and freed my previously repressed memories regarding that most difficult period in our lives.

I was guardedly optimistic about these new feelings which I saw as an emotional (albeit slight) break-through, but felt confident enough to declare that my emotions were once again under control. It was time I decided, to give Joey's Home records another try.

I walked over to the dresser and very calmly removed the envelope, containing my brother's file from the drawer, sat down on my bed and began reading the first document, [1](Joey's medical record) which in my opinion was somewhat lacking in professionalism and was obviously incomplete in its content. Strangely, there was no mention of Joey's stay in the hospital, nor were there any notations as to when they reached the decision to place Joey in the hands of a physician - nor why they finally decided to hospitalize him. There was however a typewritten notation: "2/44-Pneu." under a column named "Recommendations," that caught my attention and bothered the hell out of me. Although the notation was not initialed, it is patently evident someone from the Home's staff obviously diagnosed Joey's ailment as pneumonia sometime in February 1944, which immediately raised some troubling questions in my mind.

---

[1] –see appendix pg. 103

Number one: who diagnosed Joey's malady in February and number two, why wasn't he in the care of a physician if there were any suspicions that pneumonia was the problem? And number three, why did they determine that the possibility of pneumonia was not serious enough to merit a visit to the hospital? "What in God's name were they thinking about?" I asked myself loudly. Gone was my short-lived serenely calm countenance, and anger now seized my emotions as I grabbed the envelope and roughly pulled another document from the file; it was a letter signed by St. Agatha's Superintendent Sister M. Roberta.

[2]The letter dated March 3, 1944, was mailed to the Bureau of Child Welfare in New York City, advising them that Joey had been transferred from the Home to Bellevue Hospital suffering from quote "diagnosis, possible pneumonia." Clearly, they finally figured out that pneumonia was serious business in March, after ignoring or dismissing their similar diagnosis of February 1944.

I shook my head in disbelief at the incompetent and careless manner in which the Home's staff handled the case of a seriously ill infant. I wondered - why Joey? And how many other children met the same fate as my brother had? Rather than dwell on questions, I turned to Joey's file and extracted

---

[2] –see appendix pg. 106

another letter[3] authored by Sister Roberta (dated March 3, 1944), which was addressed to my mother.

After reading Sister Roberta's letter to my mother I became visibly upset and threw the letter across my bedroom. This was the third document I had pulled from the file and I found fault with all three. "What the hell is going on?" I wanted to know. I couldn't understand why Sister Roberta chose to advise my mother that Joey had been hospitalized suffering from (astonishingly) a "heavy cold," nor could I justify using the U.S. Mail as the carrier of the bad news.

This was another clear indication that the Home's administration did not act with the sense of urgency this situation deserved. Dispatching an emissary, from a parish near my mother's home to advise her of Joey's hospitalization was certainly a viable and more expeditious option.

"I should have asked for Joey's file forty years ago," I seethed. I would have been able to confront the Home's administration face to face I thought, though I'm not sure I would have been satisfied with any explanation they could have concocted. But then I realized that the Home would have probably refused to allow me access to their files; in as much as the Freedom of Information Act was years away from being enacted. "What a freaking nightmare," I said as I pulled another letter from Joey's file.

---

[3] —see appendix pg. 104

The next[4] letter was written on March 9,1944 by the Home's superintendent and posted to the Child Welfare Bureau, concerning Joey's final diagnosis. According to the superintendent's letter, the hospital's medical examiner had advised them on March 8, 1944, that an autopsy of Joey's body showed he had been suffering from "Tuberculosis of the lungs and Tuberculosis Meningitis and Acute Otitis Media" - obviously the Home also (incredibly) failed to detect that Joey had an ear infection. "How the hell do you miss an ear infection?" I wondered out loud. The letter goes on to say, that my siblings and I were immediately transferred from the Home to Summit Park Sanatorium of Rockland County, New York for a physical examination and tests - presumably to determine if we were also infected with TB.

I now reluctantly searched my memory and painfully recalled, that before we were spirited away to the Sanitarium, Sister Roberta asked me and my sister Hilda to come into her office and then closed the door behind her, leaving my brothers Georgie and Frankie outside in the hallway. She explained that "your brothers are too young to understand what I am going to tell you," and she went on to say, "Joey is now with God in heaven." Confused I asked her, "where is he, where is Joey?" Before she could answer, I realized she was trying to tell us that Joey was gone – Dead! The

---

[4] –see appendix pg.105

nun rambled on about tuberculosis and the Sanitarium, but in my shocked state of mind, I only half-listened to her. I turned sharply toward my sister and saw tears welling up in her eyes, so I interrupted the nun and demanded, "I want to see my mother!" Sister Roberta replied that she was attending to Joey's funeral but assured us Mom would be visiting on Sunday.

Then suddenly my sister "lost it" and started screaming with a rage she had never previously exhibited. I stood in shock as she grabbed the desk lamp smashing it on the floor, followed by the telephone and finally a chair before Sister Roberta grabbed her in a restraining hug. I remember that sometime later Hilda calmed down, but continued to cry and shiver as if she were cold – and I resumed gazing at my shoes in a shocked stupor with tears in my eyes.

Eventually the Home's car arrived and my emotionally spent siblings and I were on the move again – destination Summit Park Sanitarium.

CHAPTER 6
THE COVER-UP

My memory fails me when I try to remember any details about our rehabilitation at the Summit Park Sanitarium. I vaguely remember that we were forced (albeit belatedly) to undergo daily tests and examinations for approximately two weeks following our brother's passing. And I also recall sitting for many hours on a rocking chair in a glass enclosed room for sun therapy. I enjoyed the warm, light-headed sensation I felt as I sat resting my head back facing the blinding sun with my eyes tightly closed. The rays of the sun also seemed to warm my cold aching heart.

It was during one of those sun therapy sessions that I finally told Georgie and Frankie about Joey's fate. They handled the news reasonably well, but the sadness in their eyes belied any thoughts that they were too young to grieve. My brothers always surprised me with their uncharacteristic "inner strength", and they somehow understood that it was forbidden to engage in further discussion about Joey's fate, with me or my sister.

Unfortunately my sister was having a terrible time dealing with our loss. She was very close to Joey and I do remember how I would sometimes wake up during the night to the sound of Hilda weeping as she slept.

So although I was visibly troubled I wasn't surprised when Hilda was not discharged from the Sanitarium with me and my brothers. When our doctor advised us that Hilda would remain at the Sanitarium for further tests, he noticed the concerned expression on my face. He then reassured me with a pat on my back, and a promise that she would soon join us at the Home.

Shortly thereafter I was crestfallen once again when my mother came to St. Agatha to visit us and promptly pulled me aside to tell me, confidentially, that Hilda was taken to Bellevue Hospital (where Joey had died) after being stricken with St. Vitus Dance and Rheumatic Fever while she was rehabbing at the sanitarium. Mom asked me not to share the news of Hilda's misfortune with my brothers, because she didn't want to frighten them.

A few months later Mom came up to see us again at the Home with some sorely needed good news of Hilda's recuperation from her ailments.

She happily added that my sister was transferred to a very nice rest home in Roslyn, New York under the care of missionary nuns. I remember being somewhat placated, and grudgingly realized that I missed her more than I cared to admit.

I pushed my sad memories aside because I was getting stressed out and I also decided to continue reading Joey's file tomorrow – I needed a drink badly. And as to be expected, I had a difficult time trying to sleep that night discovering once again that you can't drown a troubled mind with booze. The next morning I was greeted with a headache, but after a light breakfast, I immediately returned resolutely to Joey's file correspondence.

I pulled out a [5]letter written by Sister Roberta dated May 2, 1945. And after I finished reading it, I was left with the feeling that her letter was suspiciously defensive in tone. Sister Roberta's letter was written in answer to a [6]letter dated April 20, 1945 which she received from a Bellevue Hospital physician's by the name of Edith M. Lincoln.

Dr. Lincoln's letter, which I also found in the file, requested "the date and strength of any tuberculosis tests that were done," before or after Joey had been admitted to St. Agatha's Home. Sister Roberta replied in her letter that "from the time of his admission until his removal to the hospital, he was

---

[5] -see appendix pg. 108

[6] -see appendix pg. 109

not visited; therefore, we did not receive consent from his mother for protective tests." "For this reason, the tuberculin test was not given here," she added.

I thought it curious that Sister Roberta found it necessary to blame my mother for the Home's failure to administer the necessary protective medical tests after we were admitted to St. Agatha's. Furthermore, I was doubtful about Sister Roberta's claim that my mother had not come to the Home to visit her children during those first three critical months. At this point, I was so frustrated that I questioned my decision to read Joey's Home records. "Do I really need this?" I asked myself.

Coincidentally, the next document from Joey's file was the[7] "Record Sheet" which produced a typewritten notation that confirmed my suspicions concerning the tone of Sister Roberta's May 2nd letter. This recorded message dated January 16, 1944 states; "Sister Roberta interviewed the mother today, she said Joseph was baptized in St. Cecelia's Church, NYC." "There it is," I yelled, "I knew she was lying!"

Clearly I deduced, the date of the record sheet's notation refutes Sister Roberta's claim - in her letter - that my mother had not visited the Home from December 1943 through February 1944, and was consequently

---

[7] -see appendix pg. 110

unavailable to sign-off for the protective medical tests. I sat back in my chair and breathe a sigh of disbelief.

I was appalled and slightly nauseated, when I realized these files contained proof-positive that an attempt had been made to cover up an act of negligence, so seriously irresponsible that it boggled my mind. To think that so many children were put at risk by being exposed to my brother and the infectious, deadly disease he carried was almost inconceivable to me.

By failing to make a conscious effort to attain parental clearance, which would have allowed my family to receive the necessary protective medical tests, the Home's administration not only endangered every child in the Home, but also deprived Joey of the opportunity to have the disease treated early on by an experienced medical staff at the local hospital. Early detection could very well have given my baby brother a fighting chance, at the very least, in his battle against the scourge of tuberculosis. If indeed it gwas necessary to have a parents signature in order to administer protective tests, I as superintendent of the Home, would certainly have seen to it that the signed documents were in my "hot little hands" – before accepting the children into the Home. "Damn it," I raged, "a bloody idiot would have had a better plan to secure the lousy parental sign-offs, than the Home's management! What the hell were they thinking about?"

After some thought, I understood clearly, why the Home's administration attempted to camouflage their culpability in the death of my brother. Obviously if they admitted mishandling Joey's case their here-to-fore unchallenged child care program would have attracted public scrutiny, and would surely have exposed the inadequacies of the program. A program fraught with questionable behavior and medical incompetence.

Hell! My brother Frankie recently admitted to me that he didn't feel like going to school one day at St. Agatha's, so he faked a stomach ache and was rushed to the hospital where his appendix was removed!

I also found it strange when my personal medical records, which I received from the Home, revealed that the doctor who performed our December 1943 "Admission Examination" found me physically malnourished. Oddly the medical records also show that one year (1948) I lost six and a half pounds and only gained a total of seventeen pounds from December 1943 to December 1948, yet I was never again diagnosed as suffering from malnutrition.

But of course I also realize that officially recorded cases of continuing and prolonged malnutrition would have damaged the Home's image, and perhaps hurt the doctor's chances of returning in the future.

A couple of days after reading how the Home tried to cover up their administration's ineptitude, I was lying on my bed staring at the wall and finally convinced myself that I had calmed my anger sufficiently. And decided I could now be trusted to make a rational decision as to what I should do with the information I had uncovered. After considering some of the options, including consulting my sister Hilda, I knew in my heart of hearts that I really had no choice but to seek accountability for Joey's death; as well as for the horrible treatment so many children experienced in the Home. An unwanted task to be sure, as I certainly did not relish the thought of dragging the skeletons from my family's collective closets.

In addition, I was also briefly concerned that any criticism directed toward the catholic Homes for children of my era, might have a negative impact on the children who live there today. However, I felt there was a better chance that an expose of the Homes' previous child-caring atrocities could improve the conditions under which the kids live in the present day catholic Home.

Ultimately I decided that the only way I could effectively accomplish this titanic task of bestowing accountability on the "guilty as sin" parties was to write a book, despite never having attempted something as difficult as writing. And writing about the terrible experiences of my youth would prove to be infinitely more difficult. I, like most Home boys, preferred burying the terrible memories of our childhood years as if the abuse never actually happened.

Other Home boys however, are resolute in their belief that they were fortunate to have received a good catholic education from the Home, and they adamantly refuse to remember that they were raised in a cold, loveless and hostile environment together with hundreds of dysfunctional children, under the auspices of cruel and insensitive sociopaths. Perhaps, it is too painful.

CHAPTER 7
THE WAR YEARS

The year was 1944 and the world was still at war in Europe, Asia, Africa, the Philippines, and back here in the United States I was fighting my own small war. But although I was taking a beating (literally) in my personal conflict, so were the hated Germans and Japanese, who were finally retreating in the wake of advancing allied armies. Thereby providing me with a glimmer of hope that Pop might possibly be discharged from the army earlier than I previously anticipated.

The world had been waging war for almost half of my eight years on this earth, and back then I sometimes pessimistically believed there was no end in sight to the damned war. However, most times I would cling fiercely to the hope that my father would return (sooner than later) to New York and rescue me from a war I had absolutely no chance of winning. I was losing battle after battle against the Prefects', nuns as well as my peers' at the home and feelings of desperation were beginning to overwhelm me.

I also recall that despite harboring emotions which were in constant turmoil during the war years, my mind never stopped scheming and searching for a way out of this unjust forced internment. An unfortunate confinement that was ostensibly designed by the State Authorities to improve the care of neglected children, but sadly had already claimed my baby brother's life and seriously impaired my sister's health.

Then one day something incredible happened to me, which I now truly believe was an inspiration from God, that eventually resulted in an appreciable reduction in the number of conflicts against my perceived enemies and significantly lowered the level of desperation in the feelings I was experiencing.

It was a day late in April of 1944 and I was playing stickball with several classmates in the Home's play yard when I fouled the Spaldeen rubber ball back, and it careened off the top of the fence bouncing crazily toward the Home's chapel some one hundred feet away. As I scampered after the ball the skies, which had been threatening all day, suddenly erupted and it started to pour. In as much as I was closer to the chapel door than any other shelter available for cover from the flash storm, I stepped into the house of God for temporary refuge and sat down in one of the pews close to the altar, where I would await the storm's end. Looking around I realized I had never been alone in the chapel, and when I attended Sunday mass, having no faith, I pretty much went through the motions of praying.

As I sat there I couldn't help notice how beautiful the statue of Mary, Mother of God appeared in the dimmed lighting of the empty chapel. I stared at the statue and was suddenly overcome with a strange peaceful feeling that left me slightly light-headed and somewhat shocked by this sensation of serenity I had never before experienced.

I repeated my visit to the chapel the very next day and again the grief and rage I had worn on my countenance since I arrived at the home seemed to subside when I prayed to the Virgin Mary. I basked in the peacefulness of God's home and was awed by the sudden awakening of my spirituality.

During that period of my bereavement, I was also very fortunate to have met the one and only person in St. Agatha's Home who showed me any compassion. Sister Antoninus, a kindly, rotund nun with a ruddy complexion and jet-black hair saw my pain and took me under her wing, while I struggled to survive that extremely difficult first year away from my home in The Bronx. She helped me greatly scholastically and tutored me throughout third grade in elementary school. She also wisely urged me to become an altar boy and was instrumental, with her influence, in my winning the appointment for the job of church maintenance boy – a major coup for a Latino in an Irish dominated society. I bristled and cursed-out the guys who irreverently referred to her as Sister Nineasses.

I soon plunged desperately and resolutely into a religious commitment, and eased my tortured mind somewhat with reassuring thoughts that Joey's innocence guaranteed him a safe haven with God in heaven. I had no doubt we would be re-united when I died.

I quickly rose to the status of number one altar boy and became a leader of the choir, as well as the Home's chorus. The chapel would become my refuge, my therapy – as well as my home. My brothers Georgie and Frankie subsequently followed my lead and inherited my position as an altar boy and church activist. They also followed my example in school, where I ranked third in my class. Georgie and Frankie surpassed my scholastic achievements with rankings of number two and number one respectively.

But although religion healed my wounded heart, and served my spiritual needs, I realized early on the necessity of forging alliances in order to allay the constant threats against my physical well being.

Thanks to my sister Hilda two upper classmen who had met her just before she was hospitalized, admired her, and eagerly accepted the role of protecting me from larger and tougher classmates. They let it be known that any violence directed toward me would be met with harsh reprisal. My sister's admirers were named Tony Alcenzio and John Nicholson, both of whom were smitten with my sister's charms and could not do enough for me. They competed for my brotherly influence in order to gain any advantage in their quest to win her attentions. I encountered Tony and Nick per chance some twenty years after they left the confines of St. Agatha's Home. Sadly, just as so many other Homeboys they were obviously underachieving.

With well-honed wits I was eventually able to compromise most of the adversity I faced in the Homes; and for a guy who was the smallest kid in the class, and of minority heritage, adversity abounded.

The schoolteachers (nuns) never requested our opinions nor our thoughts, and we learned our classwork the Home way, by memorization. The nuns would continually request the class to "Repeat after me," until they drummed the lessons into our heads – especially religious lessons. But arguably, coexisting with all the other dysfunctional children in our midst was the greatest challenge to our minds.

During recreation periods, the Homeboys were forced outdoors, by the Prefects' and we endured sub-freezing weather as well as the dog days of summer. On bitterly cold days we would often seek shelter in the unheated and unsanitary play yard toilet; where generally half the bowls were in need of plumbing and often spilled excrement and urine on the toilet floor. We sloshed through the rain with worn-out shoes stuffed with cardboard, which was useful in the event you stepped on broken glass or sharp pebbles, but certainly useless in wet weather. We wore crusty underwear and socks (with holes) which were changed once a week and wore our battered coats until the sleeves were halfway up our forearms.

Homeboys also had to contend with periodic doses of castor oil and constant applications of bug repellent lotion on our heads to combat the outbreaks of lice infestation. We slept on uncomfortable cots, in dormitories permeated with the pungent odor of urine.

The majority of the boys played football without helmets or uniforms, on a rock-hard field, and played offense as well as defense, without any "Time-Outs." The only guys in the Home who were supplied with ill-fitting football gear were the Varsity teams. We also played baseball on the same gnarled turf and most times, only three of the nine teammates were lucky enough to own baseball gloves, albeit without webbing or padding, – we called them dustpans. We also dealt with the harsh corporal punishment and the lousy food, which probably was the main reason that the Home's football teams were always out-weighed as much as thirty pounds per boy by our opponents – but we always proved to be worthy adversaries.

When I was hungry, I remember sneaking out of the dormitory during the night while everyone in my room slept, so I could raid the adjacent farms for carrots and tomatoes. It wasn't long before some of my classmates caught me munching on a carrot and thereafter I had to share the late-night raw vegetable feasts. I often quieted my growling stomach with candy or apples I would pick from the many apple trees that ringed the Home grounds.

I prayed constantly to the Mother of God during the war years and asked her for miracles that only saints receive, and I sure as hell was no saint.

However, I have always strongly suspected that the strength of mind I developed during those difficult years, which helped me survive so many dangerous adventures throughout my life, was indeed divine intervention. I continue holding onto the belief that the Virgin Mary and Joey are keeping tabs on me. No, I did not receive miracles per se, but I did receive the spiritual guidance I desperately needed during some tough times – especially when I faced life and death decisions.

As I reflect on those troubling war years in the Home, I now realize that my prior life in The Bronx was actually almost luxurious in comparison, and my family life also included that all-important ingredient called love – an emotion totally absent from our guardian's child care operation. Quite possibly they feared that showing the children some love would be interpreted as a sign of weakness.

If you asked me today to describe, in a word, my life experiences during the World War II years, my reply would undoubtedly be: Survival.

CHAPTER 8
MY CLASSMATES

It should not surprise anyone, that Homeboys were callous, insensitive racists, prone to violence and hate. Most of us hailed from the worst inner city ghettos where many parents exhibited prejudicial feelings toward people from different cultures and backgrounds. These feelings of animosity by the adults against people of diverse nationalities were naturally adopted by their offspring as the "doctrine of hate."

In the Homes' the kids found the perfect environment to vent their hatred, and not only with fisticuffs or verbal attacks against each other, but in the sports arena as well. We were fierce competitors on the gridiron, and this ferocity was fueled by the brutality of a life not of our choosing. From an age as young as six years old, Homeboys had no choice but to become mentally and physically tough, while they also progressively grew socially retarded.

The majority of my classmates (75%) were of Irish extraction, or as we referred to them, "Mics". The balance included (10%) "Wops," or Italians, several "Polacks" and a "Kraut," and I of course, was a member of the (5%) "Spics." However, we usually addressed each other with uncomplimentary nicknames. Some of the more memorable nicknames I recall were:

Pretty Boy – a good-looking Irish kid with a shock of greased-back blond hair, which he constantly combed. He was not a big guy, but he was tough as nails and would never back down from the many bullies who picked on him.

Egg Head – was the brightest kid in the class, and was also known as "Peanut," because he had a small penis. I never realized how sensitive he was about the Peanut nickname until I ran into him in The Bronx, when he was eighteen years old and approximately four years removed from St. Agatha's Home. I invited him up to my room where he startled me by opening his fly and extracting a huge dong while growling, "call me Peanut now, you bastard!" He then laughed scornfully at the shocked expression on my face, and a couple of minutes later I lied about having a date just so that he would leave.

I made certain I didn't run into that sick son of a bitch again, but I still often wonder if he wasted that God-given intellect he possessed. This guy scored 100% in virtually every exam in school while at the Home, and had the potential to reach a high station in life.

One Eye – lost his right eye as a child and wore a patch over the empty socket, which he often (to our horror) exposed. He played a mean third base for the Home's baseball team, and always played close to the base line to compensate for the missing orb. However, he had a sick sense of humor, and delighted in shocking the more weak-kneed of his classmates.

I'll never forget the night we were hanging out behind the refectory, where we would hide after throwing an occasional rock at the boys in the play yard, when **One Eye** spotted a cat. He quickly grabbed the cat, and then pulled out a long cord from his pocket and proceeded to hang the poor cat by the neck from a nearby tree. He looked at me, the only witness to the savage attack, and said laughingly, "I wanted to see if they really have nine lives."

Fat Head – always beat me out scholastically for second place in the class, and I had to settle for third place. The competition between us resulted in animosity and jealousy as well as several fistfights. I recall one of our fights in which I inadvertently punched his big head and sustained a painful hand injury.

Bull Dog – was a tough, pug-nosed Irish kid who was always fist fighting with **Hunchback** (a rawboned "Polack" who resembled a Neanderthal man) for the title of toughest kid in the class. One of their epic battles lasted, on and off, for a couple of weeks – and ended in a draw. Their fights were particularly brutal and the sickening sound of their fists colliding with flesh was frightening, but to be honest, I secretly enjoyed watching their slugfests – probably as much as the Romans loved watching the Gladiators do battle.

They were both discharged from the Home in 1949 and I never saw them again, however I did see Bulldog's name in the sports pages of a local New York City newspaper in 1996. Somehow, I wasn't surprised to read that he was training a professional boxer for a fight he eventually lost. Shortly thereafter, I read another newspaper article, which stated that Bulldog had been fired by the boxer. In light of Bulldog's violent past, I would bet the ranch that he tried boxing as a profession and failed because he led with his face – instead of his left-jab.

Mary – a popular name for the weaker and effeminate boys who were often picked on and sexually abused by the tougher kids. The tough guys usually molested the Marys' after the lights were turned off at night. You could see shadows moving in the dark, hear the footsteps and the squeaking springs. Masturbation and homosexual activity was "a given" in the Homes' and the kids accepted it as part of their day to day life, - curiously no one lost their eyesight.

In all seriousness, I still feel contrite and regret even the most minor incidents of abuse against the Marys; yet when I recently expressed as much to some ex-Homeboys, they simply shrugged it off by saying that I shouldn't let it bother me because "that's the way it was in those days, and most of us did the same thing." As always my answer to that suggestion is, "Sure that's the way it was fifty years ago, but the fact remains that abusing anyone, much less children, is terribly wrong – no matter when it occurred."

Hammer Head – was a name that described the appearance of his penis head, which was obviously the victim of a botched circumcision. He was an introvert and the only Christian in my class who was circumcised.

Hitler – the number one target of us hate-mongers was a German kid, who was always getting his ass kicked. I recall a rather vicious fist fight, which "Hitler" was winning handily until he dropped his tormentor with a hard shot to the jaw, and when the fallen fighter arose, he was brandishing the broken neck of a coke bottle in his hand. Hitler covered his face with both arms, and suffered a deep wound when his forearm was slashed by the opponent's jagged weapon. I was one of about fifteen kids who had formed a circle around the combatants, and after a moment of shocked silence at the sight of gushing blood, I ran to alert one of the Prefects. "Spud Chest" Kelly responded to my calls for help and (surprisingly) had the presence of mind to apply a quick tourniquet with his handkerchief, which stemmed the flow of blood to a trickle. Hitler was taken away never to return, and we assumed he was transferred to another Home. No one bothered to question the sudden disappearance of any kid, because the answer would always be the same – "he went home."

However, Hitler wasn't the only German to experience the wrath of the Homeboys. There was a German prisoner of war concentration camp adjacent to the rock-filled football field of St. Dominick's Home in Blauvelt, and whenever St. Agatha's played football there, we would amuse ourselves during the game by raining rocks over the fence on the prisoners who strolled within range.

Pity Boy – Was the name we bestowed on the kids who were treated specially by the Prefects and were usually assigned the job of cleaning the Prefect's room. The "wise guys" (as we called them) in my class would often speculate about the goings-on behind the closed door of the Prefect's room, when the Pity boys were being supervised while ostensibly performing their valet duties.

Beaver – was my nickname because of my buckteeth and although they made me self-conscious and I would always try to hide them, my two front teeth actually saved me from a few butt-whippings. Most fistfights were close combat affairs, where the opponents would flail away at each other's faces. In as much as my strong and sharp protuberant front teeth were the most prominent part of my face, the opponents' punches would often find them, and injure their hands in the process – ending, or postponing the fight indefinitely.

Fighting was an every day occurrence in the Homes, but I preferred the rock fights, which evened the playing field for me somewhat - while I didn't have a strong arm, it was accurate and I was very quick. God obviously blessed me with quickness to offset my lack of strength and slowness afoot. I don't remember ever losing a dodge ball contest, and I could dribble a basketball like Marques Haynes of the Globetrotters. My reflexes also helped me reduce the force of a blow from a stickball bat against my hands. I was able to time the downward swing of the bat, when I was being hit by a Prefect, and effectively ride with the blow at the instant of impact. The timing was very important, because any sign of premature movement by outstretched hands would anger the Prefect and double the punishment.

CHAPTER 9
THE POST-WAR YEARS

After World War II finally ended in August 1945, I was walking around the Home with an unmistakable spring to my step and all seemed well with my life again. Most prominently on my mind was my father, who would soon be returning to New York to liberate me from this so-called children's home, which could easily have been confused for a children's horror.

My good spirits after the war were further buoyed by a nine year old girl named Frances Jessup, who was without a doubt the prettiest girl in the Home. She was in puppy-love with me and would attend Mass every morning to see me serve as an altar boy. I remember well how she would blush whenever I rubbed her neck softly with the metal Host plate as she was receiving communion.

Occasionally I would gaze at her dreamily as she knelt at the altar like a little angel, and the priest would be forced to nudge me so I would move on to the next recipient of the communion Host.

Frances wore her long blond tresses in pigtails that framed a pretty, delicately pale face and sky blue eyes. She rarely looked into my eyes, and when I occasionally caught her looking my way, she would always quickly adjust her line of sight. To me, her shyness seemed to enhance the aura of sweetness and purity she projected.

I met Frances for the first time outside the girl's refectory while she was dumping some trash in a garbage can. I had just finished cleaning floors in the retired nun's building, and was walking past the girl's refectory on my way to the boy's side of the Home, when I spotted her. Although I was tired from working all morning, I immediately forgot about my weariness and ran to her side and offered my assistance. "Can I help you?" I asked. Startled, she turned to look at me, then blushing she mumbled: "No…that's O.K. I've finished." Then as she started to climb the stairs quickly up to the refectory I called out to her: "Hey, my name is Johnny – what's yours?" She turned her flushed face towards me ever so slightly as she continued climbing and replied: "Frances," then disappeared hurriedly through the open refectory door. I walked slowly backwards away from the stairwell and stood on my tiptoes, trying unsuccessfully to sneak another glimpse of her through the hall that led to the kitchen. Finally I turned and walked past the Administration building to the boy's side, feeling confident that Frances liked me, or she surely would have ignored my request for her name.

I proudly pointed Frances out to my mother, during one of her visits, and she was impressed. Later she asked, "but isn't she Irish?" I laughed and said, "that doesn't matter to us, she's my girlfriend." I thought Mom rather naïve at the time, but actually it was I who was naïve concerning mixed nationality relationships. Although the Homeboys constantly ragged each other about the origin of their parents or grandparents, in affairs of the heart nationality was a non-factor. Not so for the adults who were passionately opposed to any kind of fraternization what so ever with people from different backgrounds.

I was gratified that Mom had not deserted us and she came to see us every few weeks at the Home, laden with shopping bags full of food. I never did ask Mom to help us run away from the Home because I sensed that she wouldn't be able to pull it off; and besides that, she was afraid of the courts and my crazy father.

I recall that Mom paid us a visit shortly after the war's end and asked me to be sure and write her as soon as I found out when Pop was going to visit us, because she didn't want to risk any chance encounters with him. I knew then for sure what I had suspected for some time - that their marriage was over.

In any case, I gladly obliged Mom because I was not anxious to see any more of their odious confrontations. I had seen too many of their battles and believe me, they weren't pretty. I remember one fight in particular that occurred when I was about five or six years old, and I had to jump on Pop's back to stop him from physically attacking Mom – to shut her up.

Well the conquering hero returned to New York and showed up at the Home about a month after the war's end, dressed in his uniform replete with medals on his chest, and he carried a Japanese sword which he had confiscated from a dead enemy officer.

He started to tell us some war stories but I interrupted him with the only question that I wanted answered, "when the hell are we going home Pop?" I asked. He hemmed and hawed, and promised to let me know the next time he came to visit us, because he was still looking for an apartment. I wasn't thrilled about this unexpected delay but I bit my tongue and didn't say another word about it. Besides I remember thinking, today was a day for rejoicing, so I decided it wouldn't be wise to hassle Pop and get him pissed off at me. He did give me and my siblings a few bucks and eased our disappointment somewhat.

Three weeks later Pop paid us another visit at the Home and dropped a bombshell on us, when he told us that the Child Service Authority of New York had advised him that he did not have enough room in his apartment to accommodate his four children, and consequently they would only approve the release of two children. He went on to say that he had decided to firstly ask the court to give him custody of me and my sister Hilda, who had recently returned from the rest home, and when he found a larger apartment my brothers would join us.

I vividly remember that I was immediately overwhelmed with shocked disbelief at what I had just heard and my face became hot. How could he even suggest leaving Georgie and Frankie to fend for themselves as wards of the state? "No fucking way," I remember blurting out! "I'm not going to leave my brothers alone in this hell-hole," I continued. Suddenly I bolted from the visitor's room and ran into the woods behind the refectory where I often found peace away from the hectic play yard. My family followed and tried to find me, but I refused to answer their calls and leave my hiding place. When they finally gave up the search and returned to the visitor's room, I ran to the dormitory, threw myself on my cot, and cried my eyes out.

The next morning at Mass, I prayed hard to the Virgin Mary, hoping she would intercede and show me the way to cope with this cruelest of disappointments. Some hero, I remember thinking, well he wasn't a hero to me – he had lied to me and his promises were worthless. And being as I was always bragging about leaving the Home when the war ended, I was forced to think of some lame excuse so my cruel peers would not taunt me with that stupid, altered cheer leader's refrain, which went something like this:

Two four six eight

You're not going anyplace

Ten twelve fourteen sixteen

Your plans were blown to smithereens

Although I continued for quite some time to find excuses for my father's procrastination in effecting our release from the Home, I eventually saved some face by claiming that it was my decision to stay.

After the pain caused by my father's bad news had subsided, I asked my only true mentor in St. Agatha's, Sister Antoninus, to advise the social worker who was handling my case that I didn't want to leave my brothers, and that I was resigned to remain in the Home until we could all leave together. What the hell I thought at the time, I wouldn't be ten years old forever, and if I lived through the first two years I could certainly deal with a few more years of Home life if need be.

Despite my physical limitations, I began to excel in sports and my major participation in all the religious activities enhanced my status with the "powers that were". And as my star began to shine brighter, the nuns started to seriously consider me clergy material. Instinctively, I encouraged their high expectations of me, because I actually looked at the priesthood as a viable option for the future. At that time religion offered me a decent opportunity to achieve the emotional stability that I desperately needed – clearly I was really hurting.

In addition, I was fortunate that my girlfriend Frances had also remained in the Home after the war, because every time I saw her beautiful face smiling at me it made my day. When I reached the seventh grade we were allowed to dance with the girls, every now and then; it would always thrill the hell out of me when I held her hand as we slow-danced, an arm's length away from each other. I also enjoyed showing off the Lindy dance steps my sister had taught me when we lived in the Bronx.

Frances was as proud as a peacock that I was the best dancer and I really enjoyed seeing her smile and blush a bright red when I would cautiously whisper to her while we danced, that I was crazy about her. However, she was never prouder of me than the day my class was invited to Rockefeller Center in 1948 and I appeared on television; and sang that ridiculous song "I'm looking over a four leaf clover" with two other classmates.

Frances had no idea as to how important she was to my state of mind while we both languished in that loveless environment. Her long lasting

John J. Diaz

(five years) genuine affection for me was the only real stability I enjoyed in that most turbulent time of my life.

CHAPTER 10
MY PARENTS

Unbeknownst to my girl friend Frances, the fond feelings I had for her contributed to widening the chasm that my relationship with my father had become. Our relationship, which was already strained, worsened during the winter of 1948 when I learned from a girl in Frances' class that someone was being discharged from the Home within two weeks. My girl friend's classmate went on to say that the soon to be liberated young lady wished to part with her attractive winter coat, for the princely – at that time – sum of ten dollars. I remembered having seen the girl with her coat, and was certain it would fit Frances perfectly. I quickly made an offer of five dollars, through my intermediary from Frances' class, but the coat's owner insisted the ten dollar price tag was firm.

Although there was no doubt in my mind that I could have begged or borrowed five dollars from my friends in the Home, it was also obvious I would have to shake-down about seventy five boys in order to raise ten dollars. In my desperation to replace the tattered coat Frances was wearing that winter, I decided to write Pop with an urgent request for the bucks.

My father's reply arrived in seven days, which left me plenty of time to purchase the coat, but when I opened the envelope I found to my dismay that it contained a letter only – no bucks!

In his letter, Pop questioned my reason for having requested what amounted to a day and a half of his weekly salary. He also wrote that he would visit us on the following Sunday to discuss the matter.

Well I was so pissed-off that I fired off another letter to Pop and told him not to bother to visit me because I didn't want to see him. He did come to see us that Sunday – one day after the girl sold her coat and departed from the Home. But I hid in the woods behind the boy's refectory where I climbed a tall tree, for better concealment from my family, as well as for broader visibility of the Home grounds, and waited until the visiting period was over and Pop departed for his bus ride to New York City.

After the coat debacle, Pop visited the Home very infrequently, and when he did come to see us, he always brought gifts and clothes. I always felt that his generosity was a transparent ploy to try to mend our severely strained relationship. However, Pop never came back with another proposal to liberate us from the Home, and I remember that as time passed I realized it was a lost cause. So I strengthened my resolve, with the help of God, and became more confident that my siblings and I would survive the Home and all its pitfalls until I found a way out.

In retrospect, the decision to remain in the Home with my brothers was probably a huge error in judgment. I now feel strongly that had I accepted my father's initial proposal to ask for custody of his two oldest children, I would have been in a more advantageous position to pressure him into expediting the release of my brothers from the Home. In effect, I let him off the hook.

Mom and Pop emigrated to New York City's East Harlem from the impoverished island of Puerto Rico, sometime in the early 1930s during the Great Depression. They never completed grade school and did not speak a word of English when they arrived in New York, but within five years, they had taught themselves to read and write reasonably well.

I can't recall much about our lifestyle prior to my fifth birthday, however I'm certain my parents must have struggled greatly trying to make ends meet. And as the family grew, money became tighter, which naturally led to tension and numerous family arguments.

Most arguments between my parents were the result of my father recklessly squandering his earnings. Pop worked hard, but he also drank and gambled hard, and when he lost money, I would stay out of his way. I earned my money shining the shoes of neighborhood drunks, dressed in their Sunday best, at the corner of 110th Street and Lexington Avenue in Manhattan, so I never had to ask him for money to buy candy or go to the movies.

I do recall that I was not very upset when Pop went off to war, because I knew the family squabbles would cease and I would be able to do whatever I wanted. Besides, the one thing I admired about Pop was his toughness and "macho" attitude, and I was sure he would not have any problem kicking the enemies' asses – it gave me a sense of pride. Of course, I never dreamed back then that his decision to join the Army would have such a profound effect on the lives of my entire family.

My father fought in the Philippine Islands, Okinawa, and other Pacific Islands, and to his credit, he downplayed his role in the Army's victories. Although he did brag about representing his regiment in an Army boxing tournament, and was very proud of the medal he received for being the first soldier to land on the beach of some god-forsaken island the USA had invaded.

After his discharge from the Army, my father was offered a New York City subway job, which he turned down because subway employees were amongst the lowest paid New Yorkers in those days. He opted instead to accept a job at a steel foundry in Connecticut for a much higher wage.

Pop eventually re-married, as did my mother, who also worked hard sewing in the garment district factories of downtown New York City. And as I predicted when still a child in St. Agatha's Home, my siblings and I survived without my parents; not only through puberty, but for the rest of our lives thereafter.

My dear sister Hilda was in St. Agatha's Home for a period of seven years, until she graduated from High School. My brothers Georgie and Frankie lived in the Homes for a total of twelve and fourteen years respectively. I really admire my brothers for the fortitude they exhibited throughout their internment, and they never complained or expressed any bitterness.

Conversely, I railed constantly, despite having accepted life without my parents. And after spending five and a half years in St. Agatha's and three plus years in St. Agnes' Home I finally ran away. My sudden decision to leave was the result of taking a couple of shots on my butt from a Prefect armed with a rowboat oar. That night I said "basta" and walked out of the Home, without even a "by your leave."

During our adult years, my siblings and I would occasionally visit our parents. The visits were generally amiable because we never discussed our experiences in the Homes, nor little Joey's death, and my parents carried the denial and guilt of those terrible years to their graves. Ironically, they both eventually died about twenty years ago after months of battling painful respiratory ailments, very similar to the sickness my baby brother suffered before his death.

Perhaps what goes around really does come around.

CHAPTER 11
THE AGENDAS

Initially I couldn't comprehend how the State Authorities permitted the Homes to operate their child care programs with so many obvious deficiencies. But then I suddenly realized that they were actually political partners and it behooved them to work hand – in hand; in the administration of the State's multi-million dollar child care system. After all, in those days (1930s and 1940s) the New York catholic electorate was arguably the most powerful in the State, and politicians wouldn't dream of ruffling their feathers.

It also occurred to me that all the decision makers in this tragic story of child exploitation, were actually beneficiaries of the child care system as it was then structured. To prove my point I offer the following evidence, which clearly illustrates how each group realized their respective agendas.

The Parents - The Home kids' parents, most of whom were hopelessly dirt-poor, saw the Catholic Homes as a viable opportunity to free themselves of their burdensome parental responsibilities; which would allow them a much better chance to escape the squalid living conditions of their ghetto neighborhoods.

Any guilt feelings that the parents may have experienced from giving-up their children were easily erased by the blind trust they had in the clergy's ability to raise the children well and give them a good catholic education – which in my opinion was over-rated.

The corporal punishment meted out by the Home's staff was accepted without question by the parents as a necessary part of the equation. Who in those days would dare accuse, or even suspect that the politically powerful catholic church would ever resort to the use of cruel and unusual punishment to discipline the children.

I honestly believe that the majority of the parents were convinced that their agendas were morally correct, in that they were predicated on the premise that the kids would be "better off in the Homes."

The Federal Government – It is a well known fact that maintaining a strong, well-manned Military is a very high priority on the Federal

Government's list of agendas. And you can be certain that the Government was well aware that the Homeboys provided them with an abundant wealth of recruits with the necessary attributes and potential to become career servicemen.

Military personnel were allowed to visit the Home and aggressively recruit the boys over eighteen years of age, and when graduation day arrived you would always see a military bus parked on the Home grounds and eventually leave with a busload of kids bound for the basic training camps.

State and City Governments - The State and City politicians designed the Child Care system and passed legislation which facilitated the process of placing children from dysfunctional families in the Homes. They were eager to rid New York and their constituents of the petty thieves and truants who blighted the city's image, disrupted classrooms, and were potential threats to civic order. The politicians also ingratiated themselves with the politically influential catholic hierarchy by supplying them with the human resources and the capital necessary to operate their child care business.

Not surprisingly, the New York City Civil Service Agency welcomed back the tough Home graduates who applied for the dangerous and poorly paid Cops and Firemen jobs.

The Archdiocese of New York - The Roman Catholic Church was without a doubt the principal benefactor of New York's child care system.

They openly promoted their Homes for children and probably advised the parishioners who were having problems caring for their offspring, that their first and best option for resolving the situation was to send the kids to a catholic Home; where they could learn to become good and God-fearing Christians.

The Catholic Church gladly accepted the responsibility of caring for the children (the younger, the better) who were "railroaded" into their Homes, because it presented them with the opportunity to shape the kids' minds and they would be able to espouse their religious philosophy to the children with impunity.

The odds were excellent that the Archdiocese of NY would be able to realize their agenda for recruiting a percentage of the Homeboys for the priesthood as well as the Church's missionary operations. In addition, they were in an enviable position to realize another important agenda that called for the expansion of their patronage base of loyal Catholics throughout the State. And of course, the Homes were excellent training institutions for the first year nuns who were eventually assigned elsewhere.

Obviously the only losers in this grand scheme were the unfortunate and innocent children who were deprived of a normal nurturing process and the love and affection of their family; which surely had an adverse impact on the way I for one, treated my own wonderful and forgiving sons and daughter.

I am gratified to have lived long enough to finally understand that it is O.K. (and not a sign of weakness) to voice and demonstrate my feelings of love.

CHAPTER 12
THE END OF A SHAMEFUL ERA

In the mid 1970s the administrators of the Rockland County Catholic Children's Institutions unexpectedly decided to phase out their child care programs as they were then structured, opting instead to radically curtail the number of children and manage much smaller group homes. As reported by the Gannett-Journal News in July 1991, St. Agnes' Home's hierarchy claimed that the downsizing was a result of a freeze in state government funding, in addition to the rising cost of operating the Homes, which led to escalating deficits. An admission that made me wonder if a positive "bottom line" was of more concern to the Homes than the welfare of the needy children.

It is quite obvious to me now, that the principal assets of the Homes lucrative child care (minimal overhead) business were the children, and the primary benefactor of a positive "bottom line" for the Homes was the Arch Diocese of New York; who certainly needed the money during and after World War II, so they could increase the (tribute) payments to Rome and bolster the Vatican's cash-starved coffers. I for one cannot think of any other catholic organization of that strife torn era that possessed the resources necessary to remedy the dire cash-flow problems of the bankrupt Vatican – with the possible exceptions of the Arch Diocese of Boston and Baltimore.

A couple of decades after the 'Big One" the Vatican's fiscal woes had disappeared, and child care laws in the United States had become more stringent. Child abuse lawsuits against foster parents and foster homes were gaining front-page news status. The time had come for the catholic Homes to seriously determine the feasibility of continuing their child care operation unchecked. - Hence, the decision to downsize their child care programs?

I recently (June 1999) had occasion to visit St. Agatha's Home and after parking my car in their lot, I entered through the main gate unimpeded. I was amazed at how my ex-home literally shrank before my eyes. When I was a kid the grounds seemed more spacious and the buildings larger, which now makes me wonder how they managed to house up to four hundred children and upwards of fifty nuns here.

I walked slowly past the Home's main entrance and noticed that the lawn to my immediate left, once known as[8] "The Grotto", was no longer home to the much-loved statue of Our Lady of Lourdes. Gone was the Virgin Mary's life-sized likeness, as well as her shelter of vined foliage from the Grotto's front. Obviously, without the statue you cannot now refer to it as a Grotto – just another lawn. I still remember how during the blizzard of 1947 my small body was blown across this same lawn into a snow drift by a sudden gust of wind and as I fought my way to safety away from the snow bank that threatened to engulf me, I recall fearing I was a goner.

And today, a hot Sunday in June, as I call to mind that infamous storm with its angry, cold wind, which quickly numbed my youthful face and tiny hands, I shiver. I bowed my head sadly, stepped gingerly onto the lawn and the soothing feeling of the soft grass under my feet lifted my spirits as I continued walking southwest toward the football field. When I reached the field, I was surprised to see that the white yard-line markings were still visible at this time of year. And then, as if drawn by some invisible force, I made a "bee line" to the twenty yard-line near the east goal line and realized immediately why this piece of turf on the near sideline was beckoning to

---

[8] – see appendix pg. 111

me. It was the very spot on this field where I experienced fear for the first and last time, while playing a football game.

On a frigid day in late December 1943, my classmates and I were tossing a football around to keep warm when they decided to play a "pick-up" game. I was picked by the kicking team and lined up on the twenty-yard line to play the first football game of my short (8 year old) life. The only protection our bodies had against the frozen ground and our opponent's knees were our pea coats. I remember well how our first kick-off was caught, on the run, by a husky kid named Gillespie and he barreled down the near sideline past my team-mates with a scowl on his face. Suddenly I found myself in the unenviable position of being the last line of defense against this seemingly unstoppable bull, who seemed to be daring me to try and prevent him from reaching the end zone.

I was crouched low with my arms akimbo, and I could feel my heart pounding as I awaited the galloping ball carrier. Gillespie bulled disdainfully past my half-hearted attempt at an arm tackle, and shamed me into swearing to myself that I'd never be that scared again.

I soon learned that the only way I could effectively make an open field tackle was to throw a low body block at the opponent's ankles and trip them up. Obviously, it was ludicrous for a guy my size to use a head-on tackle to stop a burly run-away fullback.

From the football field I looked across a small road and saw the very familiar old handball court, which curiously has the same chips and cracks on the walls that severely altered the flight of many Spaldeen rubber balls fifty years ago. I remember how rare it was for a Spaldeen pink ball to last more than two days before they busted – they certainly were not made well enough to absorb the rigorous beating we gave them, or the cracks on our handball court walls. This may be hard to believe, but when there were no whole rubber balls available for a stickball game we made do with half a ball.

I climbed over a waist-high fence to the adjacent play yard, where six boys dressed in short pants and T-shirts, (we were too Macho to wear shorts in my day) were playing soft ball, and as I stood there watching them play my mind wandered back to the old days again. I recalled how these grounds, over fifty years ago, teemed with children of all ages, and they all had similar stories of how they were railroaded into the Home. I could almost hear them shouting obscenities above the din of so many children, as they played on these same fields where I first experienced the joy of victory as well as the bitter disappointment of defeat.

An errant throw from the softball game rolled nearby and brought me back from the past. But I didn't make a move to field the ball and throw it back to the boys, because I suddenly felt no need, at this juncture, to exhibit my fast fading athletic abilities. One of the boys passed me on his way to retrieve the ball and I asked him, "how many kids live here?" "I don't know, maybe fifty," he replied flippantly as he ran back to his game. He probably would not have believed me if I had mentioned to him that a long time ago there were four hundred children crammed into this Home.

I then continued strolling freely through the grounds and noticed that most of the buildings appeared intact, although some of them are now being utilized for different purposes. The boy's refectory, during my time, has been converted to the Infirmary and the small brick building which was once the boys hideous toilet was renovated into offices for the Human Resources Department. However, the administration building with its domed belfry, pillared entrance and drab red bricks, remains as ominous looking as ever.

I abruptly decided to conclude my visit, but on my way to the main gate I looked anxiously past the administration building entrance and gazed fondly at the building that once served as the girl's refectory. I closed my eyes and conjured up a vivid picture of Frances, my sweet childhood girlfriend, with her long blond braids, bashfully smiling at me through an open window. Hopefully I mused, she now enjoys a wonderful life and all the love she lacked as a child.

John J. Diaz

As I drove my car down the winding road, away from St. Agatha's Home, I felt as if an immense weight had been lifted from my shoulders. And I made a promise never to return to the institution that was once the scene of crimes perpetrated against thousands of innocent and helpless children.

CHAPTER 13
AN OPEN CONFESSION

Bless me my God for I have sinned, and it has been almost fifty years since my last confession.

It has taken me too many years my Lord, to shamefully admit that I was terribly wrong in my treatment of children, as well as adults, throughout most of my life. And I am sincerely remorseful for the reprehensible conduct that I so mindlessly displayed back then, especially toward the children.

Regretfully, during my long internment in the catholic Homes and for much of my life thereafter, I was also an advocate of an austere, no tolerance system for raising children, which I now totally and unequivocally reject. There is no question I could have been a much better person during my youth, and I refuse to excuse my callous behavior by pointing an accusing finger at my internment in St. Agatha's Home, where I learned how to abuse children, first hand, from my guardians. I certainly had the option to ignore the bad examples of my brutal and insensitive teachers, but since I chose to follow their lead, I admit I am equally as guilty as they were.

I was given the opportunity to prove that I had learned my lessons in unconscionable behavior well, when at the age of fourteen I was transferred from St. Agatha's Home to St. Agnes' Home for the balance of my internment. And the first work assignment I received at St. Agnes was supervising and caring for twenty-five seven-year old Homeboys. Somehow the brilliant St. Agnes administrator of that (1949-52) era, determined that the dysfunctional children would benefit from the supervision of still another dysfunctional and clueless Homeboy – me!

Although I did not treat the children with the kind of brutality which was so prevalent in the catholic Homes of Rockland County, I acknowledge that I was unnecessarily mean-spirited. And I much too often resorted to the use of profanity when scolding the kids who misbehaved.

I also clearly recall forcing the children to play football dressed only in their street clothes, and cruelly ridiculed any kid who wanted to quit playing because he couldn't take the pain of a hard block, or for failing to make a tackle. "Hell, if I could take it so could they," I told myself. Shamefully I now admit to berating them purely for my own amusement.

There were also many occasions when I would demand complete silence from the children in their playroom, after arbitrarily deciding that they were playing in an excessively boisterous manner. I must at this time confess to You my Lord, that my only real motive for insisting on a silent playroom was so I could concentrate on my reading material. Which brings to mind another haunting memory that occurred on a night during the winter of 1949, after the children I was supervising were asleep in their beds, and I was sitting in a chair, near the door in the dormitory foyer, reading a book.

I was totally engrossed in one of Jack London's wilderness adventure stories and I was fantasizing about my own involvement in the dangerous episode. Then all of a sudden I was startled by one of the kids, who was obviously sleep-walking – in as much as his eyes were closed. He walked past me slowly toward the dormitory door as if I didn't exist, and reached out for the door knob. Before he could open the door I jumped out of my chair and asked him angrily, "where the hell are you going?" The kid abruptly pulled back his extended hand and blinked his eyelids repeatedly, apparently confused and disoriented with no idea where he was, nor how he got there. So I yelled at him, "get back to bed you jerk!" Then I committed an unforgivable sin, and kicked the poor kid in the butt. I can still recall the shocked expression on his face as he quietly made an about-face and walked back to his bed, holding his behind with one hand and rubbing his eyes with the other.

I also acknowledge having avoided this inevitable and long overdue confession by deluding myself throughout the years that much of the dubious behavior I exhibited was actually well intentioned and therefore acceptable. Obviously, I was in denial.

I realize dear Lord that I cannot undo the awful sins I committed in the past, nor will I be able to fully atone for the suffering my transgressions may have caused others, but please rest assured penance will be done.

The self-imposed penance I completed this past year was very painful, and at times almost excruciating, and deservedly so. It was the least I could do to make amends for a lifetime of ignoring your commandments; and I plan to continue doing penance by fighting against child abuse.

I will be only too happy to continue preaching my credo on how to rear children to all the young adults I meet, whether they care to hear it or not. They will hear that the only way to raise children is by continually showing them love, affection, patience and tolerance. And if I am ever witness to a case of child abuse, I will use all the powers of persuasion You have graciously bestowed upon me, to convince the abusers that their behavior is unconscionable, unnecessary, and unacceptable.

I will also try to partially atone for failing to demonstrate, to my own wonderful children, all the fatherly love and affection they certainly deserved. I was sadly mistaken when I assumed that a mother's love was sufficient for any child's nurturing process – "after all," I absurdly reasoned, "I faired pretty well without anybody's love."

The truth of the matter is that I didn't even know how to accept love, much less how to show my love, and I recently expressed my thoughts in that regard when I wrote the following simple poem.

TRUE LOVE

When I was young I knew not how
to love someone with heart and soul
But now with lined and weathered brow
I've found the way to reach my goal.

Open your heart and open your mind
to one who cares without reserve
And they will then return in kind

All the love that you deserve.

J.J. Diaz

1/99

CHAPTER 14
WHERE HAVE ALL THE HOMEBOYS GONE

While writing this story and reliving the experiences of my life in the catholic Homes of New York, I felt a newly found deep respect for the Homeboys. I admire them for braving the travails of their youth, until they were released from the Home and unceremoniously dumped back into society's hands with a cheap suitcase and chump change in their pockets. They then faced an uncaring world as naïve social misfits with surly dispositions, ill-prepared for the pitfalls they would surely encounter.

I also now realize how staggering the odds were against Homeboys having a normal adult life, especially in New York City. The guys, who chose to go back from whence they came, understand very well what Frank

John J. Diaz

Sinatra meant when he sang, "if you make it there, you'll make it anywhere."

In the early 1950's New York City was ethnically divided, prejudice abounded, drugs were peddled openly, and neighborhood gangs ruled the streets. Many of us Homeboys lived in dingy furnished rooms in the vicinity of 109th Street and Amsterdam Avenue and we worked on menial dead-end jobs. We hung-out in bars and considered ourselves successful if we had a girlfriend and a couple of bucks in our pockets.

Predictably, we made many bad decisions and some of us even landed in jail, but most of us managed to survive those early years of our liberation. I really found it amazing that some of us who initially encountered severe adversity actually over-achieved and ultimately prospered.

Two such cases which stand out above the rest, were the successes of David Feliciano and Jim Rivera. These Homeboys did their "hard time" and battled back; subsequently rising to the top of their chosen professions.

David was in St. Agnes'Home for ten years and released at the age of eighteen. Kudos to David who with dogged determination beat the odds big time, graduated College and became a top executive in the then fledging computer business. He entered a strange hard world totally unprepared to fight off its hazardous temptations, and committed serious youthful mistakes that would have completely frustrated most mortals – but not David. I kept in touch with David throughout the years and witnessed his rise from the depths of life; and yet I still can't believe that despite the baggage this guy carried around, he found success in the unforgiving corporate world.

Jim Rivera played professional baseball for the Chicago White Sox in the 1950's, and in my book he ranks with Jackie Robinson and Willie Mays as the most exciting baseball players of the last fifty years. Believe me, you would pay to see Jungle Jim Rivera play ball.

Although I never met Jim, he was my favorite, because he was the epitome of a Homeboy. He played baseball fearlessly with the reckless abandon of a Homeboy, and he would sneer disdainfully at the pitchers who threw balls at his head - hence the nickname "Jungle Jim."

His life was well chronicled in a profile written by the famous sports writer Max Lerner in a Sports magazine in June 1952. For me, the most significant part of the profile was when Max Lerner wrote about Roger Hornsby's (Jim's manager) opinion concerning Jim's ability to make it in the "bigs." Hornsby told Lerner that Jim was "the best rookie I've ever had under me." But Hornsby also expressed his concern that the cruel bench jockeys would never let him forget he was an ex-convict. However when the manager mentioned the worrisome opponents' cat-calling to Rivera, he was assured by Jim that he wouldn't have any problem handling their vicious barbs. And he then asked Hornsby, "what can they do to me that ain't already been done?" "What can they say that I ain't already heard?"

Jim Rivera spent 10 years in St.Dominic's Home in Blauvelt, and just as so many of us Homeboys, after he left the institution he eventually joined the Armed Forces; but not before unsuccessfully trying to land a decent job. Having entered the Home at six years of age, Jim was obviously a naïve and impressionable teenager when he returned to the city. He had no clue, and apparently neither did the adults who were supposed to counsel him early on and prepare him for adulthood.

I also followed the same road in life after the Home as Jim did, with the exception of his experience with an unfair incarceration on trumped up charges. I even followed Jim to Chicago in 1957 (purely coincidence), but New York was my kind of town and I missed the energy and excitement of Manhattan, so I returned after only three months. I tip my hat to Jungle Jim Rivera and I'd be proud to meet him and shake his hand; and I never said that about any other man in my entire life.

Occasionally I think about the Homeboys' who frequented Shaunessy's Bar on Amsterdam Avenue and I wonder what happened to Artie Evans, Billy Herbert, the Caseys' and the Ovalle brothers. However I do know what happened to an inordinate number of guys from that gang (we called ourselves the Saints), and my heart bleeds for them because they were too young to die. We all met the tough city life head-on but somehow too many of us didn't live long enough to collect Social Security.

Guys like Jimmy Figueroa who died in his twenties, Jimmy McCann and Billy Langston in their forties, Sam Tollins and Walter Evans were in their fifties. I'm sure there are other Homeboys who never enjoyed the golden years, and for all those Homeboys who met a tragic end, I wrote this song in their memory —- rest in peace brothers.

Where have all the Homeboys gone

They found us in the ghettos of old New York
    and raised us to be men who were tough as nails
With a chip on our shoulders and a swagger to our walk
    we feared not life, nor wars, nor jails

Where have all the Homeboys gone
    Where oh where do my brothers roam
No matter where you wander I want you to know
    that Jesus is with you wherever you go

Some lay on the battlefields abroad

John J. Diaz

        some settled in towns across our land

  Others were chosen to serve the Lord

        as only we – the Homeboys can

Where have all the Homeboys gone

        where oh where do my brothers roam

I hope and pray they found a home

        cause they don't deserve to die alone

John J. Diaz

December 1999

THE END

You're Going to a Home!

APPENDIX

SAINT AGATHA HOME, NANUET, NEW YORK

Grade: CS
Name: Diaz, Joseph
Born: 9/21/41
Admitted: 12/9/43

ADMISSION EXAMINATION	RE-EXAMINED	RE-EXAMINED	RE-EXAMINED	RE-EXAMINED	RE-EXAMINED
Date Dec 10-43	Date	Date	Date	Date	Date
Height 3'4"					
Weight 23 lb					
Nutrition X					
Orthopedic 0					
Nose 0					
Throat 0					
Mouth 0					
Teeth 0					
Ears 0					
Eyes 0					
Skin 0					
Lungs 0					
Heart 0					
Glands 0					
Abdomen 0					
Genitals 0					
Nerv. System 0					
FINDINGS	FINDINGS	FINDINGS	FINDINGS	FINDINGS	FINDINGS
Malnutrit. & pediculosis					
RECOMMENDATIONS	RECOMMENDATIONS	RECOMMENDATIONS	RECOMMENDATIONS	RECOMMENDATIONS	RECOMMENDATIONS
	2/7/44—Schick-Neg. 2/44—Pneu. 3/7/44—Died at Bellevue H. 5:45p.m. Autopsy: TB Meningitis, cTB of the Lungs & Acute Otitis Media.				
Dr. [signature] Examiner	Dr. Examiner	Dr. Examiner	Dr. Examiner	Dr. Examiner	Dr. Examiner

John J. Diaz

March 3, 1944

Mrs. Lupe Diaz
878 Longwood Avenue
Apt. 3, Room 211
New York City

My dear Mrs. Diaz:

We beg to advise that Joseph was to-day taken to Bellevue Hospital as he had a heavy cold. Will you kindly go to the hospital on receipt of this letter to sign necessary papers for treatment.

       Very sincerely

       THE ST. AGATHA HOME FOR CHILDREN

       SISTER MIRIAM ROBERTA, SUPERINTENDENT

sm:cg

You're Going to a Home!

March 9, 1944

Miss Emily E. McNulty, Assistant to Director
Department of Welfare, Division of Child Welfare
902 Broadway, New York, N. Y

My dear Miss McNulty:

We herewith confirm our telephone report to Miss Quinn on Wednesday, March 8th, regarding the death of Joseph Diaz. This child died in Bellevue Hospital on Tuesday, March 7th. The Sisters visited the hospital on Wednesday, March 8th, and talked to the medical examiner who gave the result of the autopsy and it is "Tuberculosis of the Lungs and Tuberculosis Meningitis and Acute Otitis Media".

The mother was present when the child died and signed the consent for the autopsy, after claiming the body. Through some slip-up, we were not notified of the death until we called the hospital, about 7 o'clock Tuesday evening, to inquire about Joseph's condition. The Sisters waited at Bellevue Hospital until the undertaker's call for the body, and accompanied it to the undertaker's parlors, Monge Funeral Home, 1739 Madison Avenue. They tried to contact the mother all day, visited her home three times and phoned her place of business, but were unsuccessful. To-day, Thursday, the Sisters went to the funeral home and met the mother and remained with her throughout the morning. We have arranged to defray all funeral expenses.

We also took the four other Diaz children to the Summit Park Sanatorium on Wednesday, where they were x-rayed and examined by Dr. Yaeger. The chest x-ray was negative for John, George, Hilda; Frank had shadows; he will be followed withp with sputum examinations. All the children were given the Tuberculin Test but the results will not be known until Saturday.

The mother advised the Sisters that she was informed at Fifth Avenue Hospital that Frank had Tuberculosis and at that time all the children and she were x-rayed but she did not know the results. Through the advice of Dr. Yaeger, we suggested to the mother that she have a check-up, and if she could not arrange this for herself that if she would visit here some week-day, we would have this done up here for her. If there is any further information, we shall be pleased to submit the same upon advise.

Very sincerely

THE ST. AGATHA HOME FOR CHILDREN

SISTER MIRIAM ROBERTA, SUPERINTENDENT

John J. Diaz

March 3, 1944

Miss Emily I. McNulty, Assistant to Director
Department of Welfare
Bureau of Child Welfare
902 Broadway
New York, N. Y

My dear Miss McNulty:

We wish to advise that Joseph Diaz, City Bill No. A.7795, was to-day taken to Bellevue Hospital; Diagnosis, possible pneumonia. As soon as he is returned to our care, we shall advise you.

        Very sincerely

        THE ST. AGATHA HOME FOR CHILDREN

        SISTER MIRIAM ROBERTA, SUPERINTENDENT

mn:cg

You're Going to a Home!

March 3, 1944

Miss Marie Foley
Catholic Charities
485 Madison Avenue
New York, N. Y

My dear Miss Foley:

We beg to advise that Joseph Diaz, City Bill No. A.7795, was to-day taken to Bellevue Hospital; diagnosis, possible pneumonia. As soon as he is returned to our care, we shall advise you.

Very sincerely

THE ST. AGATHA HOME FOR CHILDREN

SISTER MIRIAM ROBERTA, SUPERINTENDENT

sm:cg

John J. Diaz

May 2, 1945

Dr. Edith M. Lincoln, Chief
Children's Chest Clinic, G-6 Office
Bellevue Hospital
New York 16, N. Y

My dear Dr. Lincoln:

We refer to your letter of April twentieth regarding Joseph Diaz.

Joseph was remanded to our care by the Bronx Court on December 9th, 1943. He became ill in February and was transferred to Bellevue Hospital on March 3rd, where he died March 7th. Autopsy revealed TB Meningitis, TB of the Lungs and Acute Otitis Media.

The history, as sent to us from the court, and information received from his mother, did not reveal that he was a TB contact. From the time of his admission until his removal to the hospital, he was not visited; therefore, we did not receive consent from his mother for protective tests. For this reason, the tuberculin test was not given here.

Joseph's brothers and sister are still under our supervision, all having negative tuberculin and negative x-rays.

Thanking you for your interest, we are

Very sincerely

THE ST. AGATHA HOME FOR CHILDREN

SISTER MIRIAM ROBERTA, SUPERINTENDENT

sm:cg

CHILDREN'S MEDICAL SERVICE
BELLEVUE HOSPITAL

You're Going to a Home!

NEW YORK UNIVERSITY
DEPARTMENT OF PEDIATRICS

TWENTY-SIXTH STREET AND FIRST AVENUE
NEW YORK 16, N. Y.

April 20, 1945

St. Agatha's Home
Nanuet, N.Y.

RE: Diaz, Joseph
2½ yrs.

Dear Sisters:

    In order to complete a study, I am anxious to know whether you have any record of Joseph Diaz having had contact with tuberculosis, and also the date and strength of any tuberculin tests that were done before being admitted to your institution or after admission.

    Joseph was transferred to Bellevue Hospital from St. Agatha's on 3-3-44 and died on 3-7-44 of tuberculous meningitis.

    Thanking you for your past cooperation, I am

Sincerely yours,

Edith M. Lincoln

Edith M. Lincoln, M.D.
Chief, Children's Chest Clinic
G-6 Office

John J. Diaz

THE SAINT AGATHA HOME   **RECORD SHEET**   NANUET, NEW YORK

D.P.W. _____

SURNAME Diaz, Joseph   Born 9/21/41   Adm. 12/9/43   No. S.P.C.C.

DATE	
12/9/43	Admitted today on remand from Bronx Court with brothers; Frank, George, and John, and sister, Hilda.
1/8/44	Joseph was discharged from quarantine today and placed in Mount Carmel Cottage.
1/16/44	Sr. Roberta interviewed the mother today. She said Joseph was baptized in St. Cecelia's Church, N.Y.C.
1/21/44	Sent for baptismal information.
1/25/44	Received baptismal certificate today. He was baptized in St. Cecilia's Church, 120 East 106th St., N.Y.C. on November 29, 1942.
3/7/44	Discharged today. Died at Bellevue Hospital at 6:45 p.m.

You're Going to a Home!

    Frankie   Hilda   Georgie   Johnny

ST. AGATHA'S GROTTO

ABOUT THE AUTHOR

John J. Diaz was born on June 25, 1935 in "Spanish Harlem", New York City and was raised in the catholic Homes of Rockland County, New York. He continues to reside in his beloved native state and vows to remain a New Yorker for life. John proudly claims that, "This is the most vibrant and exciting state in the USA, and its beautiful mountain ranges, cities and quaint towns are second to none."

Mr. Diaz retired from business in 1996 and is now pursuing careers as an artist and a writer. He wants to concentrate on art for a year, and plans to write a book about his dangerous adventures as a bachelor in the Big Apple, during the wild nineteen sixties and seventies.

Lightning Source UK Ltd.
Milton Keynes UK
21 February 2011

167908UK00002B/324/A